June 1995

Dearest Carolyn –

"Who loves a garden
finds within her soul
life's whole...."
May you always have a
garden in your life!

With love,
Valerie

THE WAYSIDE GARDENS COLLECTION

The CONTAINER GARDEN

THE WAYSIDE GARDENS COLLECTION

The
CONTAINER
GARDEN

A Practical Guide to Planning & Planting

Thomasina Tarling

John E. Elsley, General Editor for The Wayside Gardens Collection

 Sterling Publishing Co., Inc. New York

Library of Congress Cataloging-in-Publication Data Available

2 4 6 8 10 9 7 5 3 1

Published 1994 by Sterling Publishing Company, Inc.
387 Park Avenue South, New York, N.Y. 10016

The **Wayside Gardens** Collection edition

© 1994 Conran Octopus Limited
The original edition first published in Great Britain by
Conran Octopus Limited
37 Shelton Street, London WC2H 9HN
Text and original planting schemes © 1993 by Thomasina Tarling
Design and layout © 1993 by Conran Octopus Limited
Distributed in Canada by Sterling Publishing
c/o Canadian Manda Group, P.O. Box 920, Station U
Toronto, Ontario, Canada M8Z 5P9
Printed and bound in China
All rights reserved

American Project Editor	Hannah Steinmetz
Project Editor	Jane O'Shea
Project Art Editor	Ann Burnham
Editors	Carole McGlynn
	Caroline Davison
Designer	Alistair Plumb
Picture Researcher	Jessica Walton
Production	Julia Golding
Illustrators	Shirley Felts
	Ann Baum
	Christine Wilson
	Nicola Gregory
	Michael Shoebridge

Sterling ISBN 0-8069-0843-2

FRONT JACKET *An engaging collection of terra-cotta pots;* Buxus sempervirens 'Suffruticosa' *is in the foreground with* Salvia officinalis 'Purpurascens' *and* Ruta graveolens *embroidered with* Verbena 'Sissinghurst.'

BACK JACKET *An exuberant collection of sun-loving plants.*

PAGE 1 *A summer bedding combination of petunias with an ornamental cabbage.*

PAGE 2 *A group of container-grown plants includes tender* Bougainvillea *and trailing* Campanula *with formal evergreen topiary.*

RIGHT *In this tiny courtyard garden flowering plants include yellow* Abutilon *and purple* Heliotropium.

CONTENTS

CONTAINERS FOR ALL GARDENS

Almost no space is too small for at least one plant in a pot, while the grandest gardens in the world use containers for enhancement. In between lies a thrilling jumble of pots, urns, tubs, boxes, baskets, sinks, cisterns and troughs, all awaiting a cornucopia of plantings. Such superb pots and urns have been produced for generations, themselves works of art; the challenge of blending them with enhancing plant material is irresistible.

The author's very small garden in mid-summer. Against a background of lush foliage are Fuchsia 'Thalia,' Impatiens *(New Guinea hybrid),* Cordyline australis *and a standard* Argyranthemum frutescens *next to* Pittosporum *'Silver Queen.' A pair of standard* Cupressus glabra *frame a seat backed by* Berberis *'Rose Glow' with a blue-glazed pot of* Hosta *'Temple Bells' at its feet.*

*A row of huge classic terra-cotta pots holding young lemon and orange trees (*Citrus limon *and* C. mitis) *evokes a Mediterranean mood.*

The possibilities offered by container gardening today are tremendous and the enjoyment to be derived from it is immense. This form of gardening is at the same time practical, skillful, rewarding, infuriating and enormous fun, but it is vital to face up to its limitations and to be realistic about its possibilities: gardening within a restricted space is quite different from gardening in an unfettered one. Not only are contained plants unlikely to grow to 150 feet or spread to cover an acre of garden, but the very placing of a plant inside a container makes it more visible, vulnerable, subject to a different discipline and somehow more special.

The earliest gardeners treated only their most precious plants thus: the orange trees flowering delightfully in their decorated pots were the very pinnacle of horticultural achievement. Priceless tulip bulbs were given the most superb pots in which to display their charms; lilies emerged from marvelously sculpted containers. In topiary, the whole balance and line of the standard bay tree, so crisply clipped and trained, depended on the box or pot

holding it. Plants which themselves have a degree of artificiality generally make the best candidates for containers: tulips and lilies, tiny fairy alpines, camellias, Japanese maples, hippeastrums, phormiums, yuccas and pansies—the list is extensive, and a moment's thought will always add to it.

Choosing the ingredients

All gardening is about choice, but nowhere is this so important as in container gardening. We choose not only the container, the plants and type of soil to put inside it, but also the position, aspect and angle in which it stands. Because of this lack of restriction, we must be prepared vigorously to reject the ugly,

the unsuitable, the unworthy and the unhealthy. The range of containers available is so huge, and encompasses almost as many disasters as successes, that it behoves beginners to be ruthlessly selective. Better one decent-sized pot than a pair of mingy ones, for example; better a good, plain terra-cotta, which will weather and improve with age, than a plastic imitation urn which will not. If we make a mistake in ordinary gardening, there is generally something coming along behind it which will take over, or at least soften the blow. When contained, a mistake glares, so choose pots and plants with care; discard or promote with equal vigor, and vow to improve all the time.

Grandeur and simplicity combine to form an inspiring garden scene. The formal container planting of standard bay trees (Laurus nobilis) in wooden barrels and a topiary box (Buxus sempervirens) echoes the classical stone pillars and is softened by a tank of water lilies (Nymphaea alba).

OPPOSITE *Every principle of harmonious grouping is embodied in this exuberant summer planting scheme. Height is supplied by the spiky leaves of* Cordyline australis; *spread and foliage contrast from* Helichrysum petiolare, *while the trailing pelargonium and fuchsia provide flower color and delicacy of form. Such generous planting requires constant watering and feeding.*

RIGHT, TOP *Triumph of topiary in a single container: this standard* Cupressus glabra *provides a stylish feature all the year round. It is underplanted with* Begonia semperflorens 'Cocktail' *but in colder seasons the tender begonia could be replaced with winter bedding such as Universal Plus pansies or heathers.*

RIGHT, BELOW *Such an original container as this is best complemented by a shapely plant such as this* Francoa.

The importance of scale in this style of gardening cannot be overestimated, since much of the success of container planting lies in the correct use of scale. Meanness is one of the cardinal sins of horticulture, and never more so than in choosing and planting for pots. In a small courtyard, it is preferable by far to choose one giant, handsome urn, plant it generously and withdraw. Where choice is restricted by cost rather than space, splurge on size, simplicity and impact; eschew daintiness, bittiness and over-ornamentation. As with all fields of design, there are always those rare souls born with a naturally impeccable sense of style, but for the rest of us it is important to train the eye and our taste will tend to improve with practice. Visiting open gardens and local flower shows, as well as looking with a critical eye at some of the better municipal schemes in planters, all help to develop a visual sense.

Caring for your contained plants

Maintenance is the Achilles heel of container gardening. Too many people spend hours selecting good pots and plants, put them all together with care in a well-chosen position, then retreat with a contented sigh. Some weeks later, they wonder why everything therein has died, withered or dropped. The owner of the most spectacular roof garden I have ever visited confesses he often walks around with a watering can in one hand and an open umbrella in the other. So do not embark upon container gardening without a determination to tackle the after-care, feeding and watering as often as necessary. If it is your own garden, and the plants your friends, you will not grudge the maintenance; it is one of the great pleasures that gardening offers.

I have a theory that all forms of container garden deserve a great many "treats," countering the restriction on space with as much extravagance as the budget will allow—and, frequently, more. Since you are constrained and cannot plant the rolling acres you might dream of, nor even a billowing, picture-book cottage garden, you are thereby entitled to indulge in impulse buying. This might include all manner of specimen plants to give height and instant joy to your courtyard, such as the extravagant standard fuchsias, pouring forth their ridiculously

ABOVE *The author surrounded by the flowers and foliage of her contained garden in summer. Roses include* Rosa *'Aloha' and* Rosa *'Margaret Merril,' and the main shrubs are* Acer palmatum dissectum, Berberis *'Rose Glow,'* Arbutus unedo *and the pair of standard* Cupressus glabra.

LEFT *A well-chosen group of terra-cotta forms a pleasing variety of plant shapes and textures. The main players include:* Osteospermum *'Cannington Roy,'* Helichrysum petiolare, Convolvulus mauritanicus, Brachyscome iberidifolia, Diascia, *a dwarf* Argyranthemum frutescens *and* Sempervivum tectorum.

frilly explosions of color with prodigal splendor. Half-standards have a stumpy charm all their own and are invaluable for the stylish roof or balcony garden. In a grouping of different-sized containers, they provide valuable height; set in a low, clipped hedge in a raised bed, they are elegant and interesting; placed either side of a low doorway, they can look excellent, without the daunting formality of full standards. Of course, patience is the cornerstone of gardening, and it is perfectly possible, and great fun, to grow our own standards and half-standards by judicious training of suitable shrubs and trees; but if we can control a space only 20 ft. × 15 ft., we deserve to make it look wonderful *now*.

Container gardening is by no means limited to small spaces or city use. For these, it may be the only form of gardening and therefore doubly important, but containers are also used to enhance the very largest and grandest gardens. It is not difficult to recognize the role of container gardening in its many aspects. The next step is to become better at doing it, in whatever form most suits you, bearing in mind that it is important only to undertake a style of gardening that blends with your life. I hope to discuss all aspects of this art in practical, horticultural and ornamental terms; to give some idea of the effects to be attained, the improvements to be made, the challenges to be overcome, and the fun to be had.

An example of stark simplicity at its most impressive: this pair of plain terra-cotta pots frame an arch in the hedge, leading to another part of the garden. The plain white petunias show up dramatically against the dark yew hedge and draw the eye far more effectively than a multi-colored scheme.

PRACTICAL CONTAINER GARDENING

Before you embark on any form of container gardening, give the whole enterprise some thought. Always make sure the container is the best you can afford and that the selection and management of plant material, planting medium and situation are of the highest standard you can provide. One of the joys of gardening is the way in which plants work with you, improving all the time, arranging themselves in better ways and shapes; covering blank walls; adding to the sum of their parts—all you need to contribute is a modicum of care and attention and judiciously exercised control.

Neatly clipped box shapes and arching leaves of Phormium tenax 'Yellow Wave' are used to highlight a successful mixed garden planting. Their simple solidity provides a balance for the colorful and ebullient planting behind.

Choosing containers

Terra-cotta is a natural material that blends readily with plants. These handsome clay pots form a harmonious group either side of the pedestaled statue. The bold, shapely foliage of the Fatsia japonica *'Variegata' contrasts with the delicate flowers of* Argyranthemum frutescens, *the daisy bush and complements the* Zantedeschia.

In effect, a container can be anything that will hold soil, from an old boot to a pair of eighteenth-century lead urns. In between these two extremes there is a vast array of pots, urns, boxes, sinks and troughs, all available in many different sizes and materials, and most local garden centers or pot shops have a wide selection from which to choose. Superb pots and urns have been produced for generations in different styles and materials, and the challenge of planting them is irresistible.

Your choice will be dictated by many factors—space, budget and personal taste—but it is always vital to match the type of container to its setting. A formal, period doorway calls for a completely different response from a cottage garden, for example. And just as some types of container complement different styles and periods of house and look their best in certain situations, some plants have an affinity with a particular shape of pot (see page 78).

Generally speaking, natural materials make better partners for plants; these include wood, stone, terracotta or lead in all their myriad forms. If you are fortunate enough to find or inherit an antique copper, its subtle coloring and classic lines make it an ideal container. There are also some very good imitations around and these may suit your budget better, while retaining the visual appeal and suitability of the original material. Plastic is, however, always best avoided. Traditional urns are made not only in real stone but also in reconstituted stone and in stone and fiberglass mixtures. Modern copies of antique containers are often produced in lighter-weight materials, such as fiberglass, and these are ideal for the roof or balcony garden, where weight is nearly always an important consideration.

Terra-cotta pots come in every imaginable shape and size and always look the perfect foil for plants, while the recently imported glazed Chinese and Thai

RIGHT The shiny, galvanized bucket and the shallow, rustic basket make unusual containers for the glorious annual, Portulaca grandiflora *(Sundance Series), with its feathery leaves and brilliant-colored flowers.*

FAR RIGHT Large, dramatic containers such as this oil jar can be left empty and treated as sculpture or be planted with an upright or a trailing species, as here. The blue-gray foliage of Lotus berthelotii, *with its lobster-claw flowers, shows up strongly against the shape of the pot.*

pots add an extra dimension to the range. Besides traditional hanging baskets you can now find decorative wirework stands and baskets, either original or modern copies. Wood is generally used for window boxes, half-barrel-shaped tubs and Versailles tubs, but some of these can now be found in good imitations too. Sinks, troughs and cisterns have particular, and more limited, appeal which may suit certain situations, while fun containers can include all manner of recycled objects such as chimney pots, galvanized buckets, old tires and bathtubs.

There are occasions when some specific plant or position will demand a particular type of container. The roof garden with weight problems cries out for lightweight fiberglass; the water garden, too, can be created entirely from fiberglass, terra-cotta being too porous. In any area vulnerable to the public, only the heaviest, most immovable giant stone urn has a chance of surviving without being either stolen or

vandalized. In urban situations, sharp corners may present a hazard, and large, round modern containers will have to be used. Next to a building where the architect has deliberately used brick or stone of a particular color, or the walls have been painted in a demanding shade, it makes sense to select containers as close in material, tone or color as possible. If every feature of a modern building has been painted black, a black or dark gray container planted with, say, golden foliage plants for contrast would make an appropriate choice.

If you are creating your first container garden, do not necessarily buy the first attractive pots you see when you visit the garden shop. Walk around and compare sizes, shapes and prices, and consider the suitability of the material to your setting. Look for the bargains: chipped pots and damaged urns are often sold for half-price and some, especially those that have sat around acquiring good algae, are a good buy. Once they are planted you will not notice the chips, and a cracked pot can be repaired with several twists of sturdy wire or strong contact adhesive, and will give years of faithful service.

LEFT *This large decorative pot in earth hues supplies both strength and contrast for* Euonymus fortunei *'Emerald 'n Gold' with the distinctively colored* Euphorbia amygdaloides *'Rubra.'*

BELOW *A handsome, fiberglass Ali Baba jar throws the foliage of the surrounding plants (hostas, foxgloves,* Alchemilla mollis, Rheum *and* Onopordum*) into relief, and has all the more impact for being left unplanted.*

FAR LEFT, TOP *The solidity of this plain wooden barrel is ideal for a standard shrub. Its somber color is a good foil for the bright flowers of* Lantana camara.

FAR LEFT, BELOW *Mophead hydrangeas need a generous-sized pot to meet their watering and feeding requirements.*

LEFT *A spring planting, in an antique "copper," of double early pink tulips (*Tulipa *'Peach Blossom') looks effective against the variegated holly.*

Choosing the plants

Plants with strong, dramatic shapes need to be positioned with care. In this informal group of pots around a sitting area, the brilliant orange-red trumpets of Fuchsia *'Thalia' echo the leaves of* Phormium tenax *'Sundowner' and are balanced by the spiky* Cordyline australis *and Chusan palm,* Trachycarpus fortunei.

Our spirits are always lifted by the sight of growing things, and when plants are concentrated, as they are in containers, their impact is even stronger. Just as tumbling hanging baskets brighten many city streets in summer, a wooden tub crammed with cheerful annuals placed beside a front door gives a friendly welcome; well-filled window boxes give an instant lift; and a huddle of sweet-smelling plants in varied pots softens the line between paving and lawn. Your choice of container plants will be largely influenced by personal preferences, but the selection needs to be made with an eye both for the plants' suitability for the type of container and how well your chosen species will look together.

One glance at any nursery catalog or glimpse into a garden center will reveal the vast array of plants awaiting us, and this can be daunting. To simplify matters, you should bear in mind several basic considerations that will influence and immediately restrict your choice. Ask yourself whether you want to create a formal or informal effect; whether you intend the planting scheme to be a permanent one or one that changes with the seasons, or a combination of both types of planting. Finally, you have to bear in mind the scale, and rate of growth, of the plants that you are considering for your containers, and choose them to suit the space that you have available in your garden.

If your aim is formality and enhancing a period or classical scheme, you will choose plants, as well as containers, in this mode. You may have a pair of containers for either side of the front door, or a single large urn to stand at the head of a flight of steps leading to a structured garden: for both of these examples, evergreens, possibly clipped or topiarized, will strike the right formal note. Or do you want your planted container to strike a cheerful chord against a dark yew hedge, where the design is formal but nevertheless requires some bright color to make an impact? This might call for a classic urn with massed tulips for spring, followed by heliotrope underplanted with silver *Helichrysum petiolare*.

Alternatively, if informality is your style, you will lean toward the colorful, the fanciful, the overflowing and the spreading. If containers provide your sole garden and you want them to be cheerful, colorful and everlastingly good-looking, you will want to choose seasonal bedding, combining colors you prefer and probably changing it three times a year, using spring bulbs, then summer mixtures followed by a foliage shrub, trailers and winter-flowering pansies. If your informal containers are large, you might mix permanent and bedding plants, aiming for a handsome shrub or small tree, underplanted with lilies, say, and adding petunias or verbenas for summer. You might want a huge, cheerful hanging basket, crammed with color and foliage, to hang dramatically against creeper-covered walls. Small terra-cotta pots filled with bright pelargoniums would be a simple but uplifting antidote to an unadorned balcony.

Permanent planting schemes will include trees, shrubs and climbers whose presence you want to count upon; temporary dwellers will flit past, colorful, evanescent, exotic, removable. There is usually room for permanent plants and annuals in both a formal plan or an informal scheme. But the distinction between the formal and informal styles should not become blurred and you should always pay heed to the setting—a big, blowsy mass of mixed summer bedding, however cheerful, will not look right

outside an elegant period town house. Conversely, a handsome terra-cotta pot holding a magnificent *Magnolia grandiflora* or a grand clipped bay tree looks pretentious beside a modest cottage. You can mix formal and informal only where there is a certain distance between them; you can have a formal arrangement outside your front door and an informal group on the terrace at the back of the house, for example, or formal on the terrace and clusters of pots at the edge of the lawn beyond.

In front of the Wisteria, *the* Argyranthemum *daisy flowers contrast with the lime green of* Nicotiana *and the deep purple of* Heliotropium *with the soft mauve of* Brachyscome *spilling down.*

RIGHT *The pair of standard* Lantana camara *flank the doorway, while the cheerful pots of pansies, petunias, heliotropes and small daisies, including* Brachyscome, *brighten the stone courtyard.*

BELOW *This lead planter provides a superb showcase for the spectacular but tender* Brugmansia suaveolens *(syn.* Datura suaveolens*) and a variegated, cut-leaved* Pelargonium *at its base. Its placing over a manhole cover illustrates the use of a well-planted container as a cover-up.*

Another vital aspect to consider when choosing plants is that of scale. Plants that are well nourished and watered are going to grow; some do not improve with age and need constant cutting down in order to refurbish themselves. Unless you are prepared to prune ruthlessly (see page 32) to keep the scale of your plantings in balance, or unless you have a large space in your garden where a tree or shrub can go once it has outgrown its useful life in a container (see page 31), always pay heed to a plant's maximum height, spread and speed of growth. *Eucalyptus gunnii*, for instance, starts off as a small, silvery accent with charming frilly leaves, but it can shoot up into a serious tree almost as you turn your back. Similarly, the heart-lifting *Robinia pseudoacacia* 'Frisia,' brilliantly golden against the spring sky, can darken an entire house within four years.

If you are planting climbers, or wall shrubs, be warned that most true climbers have minds of their own and seriously wandering hands. The creeping, hairy leaves of *Actinidia chinensis*, for example, are only the beginning, and *Vitis coignetiae*, the giant-leaved ornamental vine, can hurl itself up trees and into next-door's windows without pausing for breath. So consider well before you plant a climber, and prepare your wall by stretching wires across it, or by using vine eyes or wall nails if the climbing plant is not self-clinging.

Finally, it has to be said that there are certain plants which simply do not care for container life at all. They may allow you to confine them for a brief sojourn, even fooling you into thinking you have conquered them—but sooner or later they will cease to thrive and will start to look miserable. Many deciduous clematis fall into this last category: I have tried several cultivars, but they all faded away after two or three years, producing fewer flowers each succeeding year, despite my desperate pleading and feedings. Roses also have a tendency to dwindle (see page 31) as do euphorbias and even some hellebores. *Ajuga* seems not to care for container life either. But that still leaves an astonishing range of plants that do thrive in the confines of a container from which to make your choice.

Having made a selection of candidates that are suitable for the space and the setting, it is important to put together plants which have some affinity, both in looks and habit—a rampant grower with smothering tendencies will not make a happy partner to a delicate alpine. Hostas do not nestle comfortably against pelargoniums, nor rhododendrons with clematis. The echo principle should guide you here: if you study successful mixed plantings, both contained and loose, you will notice shared characteristics or counterpoints—the flowers of one plant echo the foliage of its neighbor; a spiky centerpiece calls for some roundness below; the bright blue flowers of an *Agapanthus* rise above a deep blue glazed pot. If you plan to have a shrub with a climber growing through it, choose a pair which can be pruned together, or which flower compatibly.

The writer and gardener Vita Sackville-West used to walk around her garden at Sissinghurst, Kent, in England, picking flowers and foliage from one plant to try against other plants before moving them to a new position or embarking on planting a new area of the garden. Most of our nurseries now have such splendid collections of herbaceous and annual plants, of alpines and small shrubs, that I would advocate walking round and setting up an imaginary box or tub before making your final purchases. It will be both interesting and instructive to see what plants best complement each other—and you may have some surprises.

Suppose you have a single terra-cotta pot that will live on a sunny balcony or terrace: start with a *Cordyline*, plain or colored, surround it with trailing pelargoniums, add some small pots of ivy—and you have a container garden. But while you wander round the nursery, look at the shrub section, find something whose foliage appeals to you—a *Pittosporum tenuifolium* 'Silver Queen,' an *Elaeagnus*, a *Hebe*, an *Ophiopogon*—visualize it with any of the bedding plants so temptingly laid out around the corner, and try to build up a mixed planting whose foliage blends with the flowers to produce a harmonious scene. If there is a shrub you particularly admire, give it a pot to itself (after reading the instructions on the label to check that your situation is suitable) and add nothing more than trailing lobelia, which will flower all summer and can easily be replaced for the following year.

RIGHT *The elegant, weeping standard* Fuchsia *'Piper' is balanced by a much smaller* Fuchsia *'Nellie Nuttall' tucked at the base. The plain shape and rounded lines of the pot that holds them is a good foil for their frilly exuberance.*

BELOW *Hostas in pots are the strawberries and cream of container gardens. Here* Hosta fortunei aureomarginata *gleams against the dark foliage of box, and the plant flourishes in a good, solid terra-cotta pot on the brick terrace.*

Planting containers

When it comes to planting your containers, paying attention to basics will ensure that your plants have a healthy start, and this is especially important if you intend their stay to be long-term. Guidelines for planting are given below.

The planting medium

Ordinary soil is not generally suitable for container work. But if you have a large garden, some of your surplus soil can be mixed with peat moss, or peat substitute, and coarse sand in roughly equal quantities, adding nutrients in the form of slow-release fertilizers in the recommended proportions. If containers are your only form of garden, the very best compost is to be found, ready-mixed, in your local garden center or nursery, packed in manageable bags and probably costing far more than you consider reasonable. However, regard it as the foundation of the enterprise, and do not be tempted to skimp. The larger your bag, the cheaper the compost becomes, so either share or store it. It will last for a season as it is, and extra fertilizer can be added if it is not used for years. If your intended plants are lime-hating, choose the specially formulated acidic compost; eschew mushroom compost (which is alkaline) and try to water with rainwater only.

If you are planting a tall container, use a larger quantity of gravel or drainage material at the bottom of the pot. In a large raised bed requiring masses of soil, your mixture can contain a greater proportion of ordinary garden soil or, if buying a ready-mixed compost, select the cheaper form of bagged compost for the lower level, and the best quality for the top 16 in. of soil in the bed.

There are also soil-less composts, which have the advantage of lightness, both to transport and *in situ*. However, I personally find that they tend to dry out too fast and are almost impossible to re-activate after this has happened, so I do not use them in general and long-term container planting.

Drainage

All plants require drainage and provision must be made for it. Ensure that there are adequate holes in the bottom of your container, then use something to prevent those holes clogging up with wet soil. The usual solution is a layer of clay crocks (from broken flowerpots). An alternative, or in some cases an additional, drainage layer consists of coarse, washed gravel or commercial water-retentive granules. Where the container is to be used on a roof or balcony, I first place over the hole a thin layer of

Planting a mixed container

Put a layer of crocks or gravel over the drainage hole. Follow this by a layer of chopped-up sod, leaf mold or moss, before half-filling your container with compost. Leave space in the middle to accommodate the substantial rootball of your main plant comfortably. Place the tree or shrub in it and back-fill with more soil, firming the plant in as you go. When doing a mixed planting, trees generally go in first, followed by shrubs, then bulbs and corms, with bedding plants added at the final stage.

Firm everything in well with your hands after planting, so that there are no air pockets around the plants' roots. Leave enough space at the top for watering.

"liner" material sold as weed suppressor in garden centers, or as padding in carpet shops: a fine fiberglass composition, permeable by water. This prevents too much soil leaking through and staining the paving beneath. It is not essential to do this for containers used within a garden, however.

Planting

While shrubs and trees need plenty of space, bedding plants seem to enjoy a huddled life—certainly the crowded window box, with every occupant jammed against another, does better than one with an expanse of empty soil. So if you think you have more seasonal bedding plants than can possibly be crammed in, do not despair: lean down and force them in. When planting bulbs, put them fairly close together, staggering where practicable, some below others, depending on their size, height and flowering times. Massed bulbs have far greater impact than mingy rows, and most look prettier emerging from greenery or foliage.

Planting a container or a window box from scratch gives you a chance to shuffle the plants about for best effect; to build up your compost gradually; and to settle everything in firmly. Adding or replacing existing plantings once some growth has been made is trickier and requires dexterity as well as firmness. Scoop out some root space, making sure the hole is deep enough, and put in the new plant with some weight behind it, before watering the entire planting thoroughly to settle it in. Always firm new plants in well, since they do not care for pockets of air around their roots. Existing plants can be held together, propped back with a stick or pulled back out of the

A long-lasting planting of Hebe × andersonii 'Variegata,' Erica carnea 'Springwood White,' the dwarf conifer Cupressus elwoodii, Hedera colchica 'Dentata' and pale Universal Plus pansies.

Planting a window box

Lay the squares of liner (if you intend using them) directly over each hole, and place crocks, stones or ready-made drainage material carefully to a depth of at least 2 in., followed by a layer of compost. Place any permanent or accent plants in position to see how much depth they require, and then add or subtract some of the first soil layer. If bulbs are to go in, lay them in position and surround them with compost, then continue with bedding plants, firming lightly as you go, until the box is full.

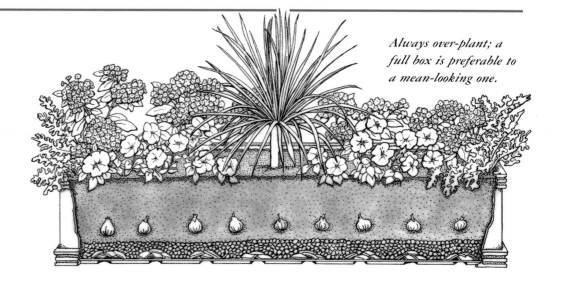

Always over-plant; a full box is preferable to a mean-looking one.

way with a piece of wire, while filling in, and allowed to flop back when the job is completed. Sometimes a little judicious pruning is necessary to make room for the newcomer. If you know you intend to insert an additional plant into a mixed planting at a later time—perhaps a tender subject in spring when your main planting is being done in autumn—it can be helpful to put in an empty flower-pot to keep the space open. This can then be pulled out for the new plant to be slipped into its hole.

Always look for the plant's best side when putting in a large or "specimen" one—all aspects are slightly different, so arrange the best to coincide with your viewing point. If you are planting a tree alone, such as putting a standard bay tree (*Laurus nobilis*) into a Versailles tub, some experts recommend putting a thick layer of gravel or sphagnum moss over the topsoil to retain moisture.

Moving pots

Where possible, plant large pots in their permanent home because they are extremely heavy and difficult to move once filled. However, there will always be occasions when large containers have to be moved to a different position, and here a strong friend comes in useful. Round pots, even quite large ones, can be spun by lifting one side only and rotating them along carefully and slowly.

Other shapes of container can be dragged along on a burlap or similarly sturdy sheet. Alternatively, they can be raised onto pre-built wheeled platforms —either home-made or bought—and moved to their new position. It is very important that you make sure the wheels have a locking device—the thought of a runaway giant stone urn does not bear contemplating.

*Moving this precious terra-cotta pot to provide a degree of protection for the well-grown bay tree (*Laurus nobilis*) will require skill.*

Planting a hanging basket

Start with sphagnum moss, making sure it is damp, and put a thin layer on the very bottom; add a shallow layer of compost, then gently insert your small trailing plants through the lowest holes, covering their roots with compost. Continue to line the basket with moss as you progress upward, always putting the moss in before the compost. Firm the small plants as you go, giving the basket a shake to settle everything down. When you reach the top, insert a few larger plants, allowing room for the hanging chains.

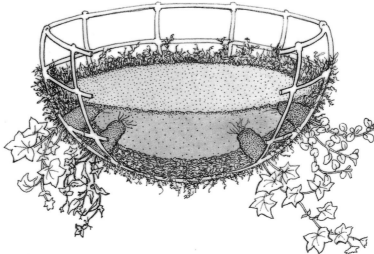

Unless you can hang your basket above a planting bench low enough for you to reach comfortably, set it on an upturned bucket or pot to plant. Once the basket is full, give it a gentle but thorough watering, until water trickles out all around; let it drain before you hang it.

Care and maintenance

Maintaining a container garden in pristine condition is essential. The very fact that everything grown in containers is totally at our mercy makes care and control imperative. While a larger, conventional garden can be left to nature for a time without suffering too much, there is no sadder sight than a pot full of decaying plants and dried-up soil. However, the appeal of container gardening is enhanced by the small amount of effort called for to achieve astonishingly effective results. The equipment needed is minimal and the main requirements are regular watering and feeding, especially in the summer months, timely pruning to keep trees and shrubs looking their best and protection against bad weather and pests. If your only garden lies contained before you, gazing reproachfully through the windows, it should be both a duty and a pleasure to make sure it looks attractive all year round.

Essential tools

Besides patience and dedication, the only things a container gardener needs are a watering can with a detachable rose (or a hose with adjustable outlet) and a few tools, so treat yourself to the best you can afford. A hand trowel and fork are essential; choose stainless steel, with wooden handles, for preference. A dibble, with a pointed end, comes in handy for inserting small seedlings or adding to a window box or hanging basket. A hand fork on a long handle is immensely useful for anything more than a single pot; these come in various lengths and the most useful material is lightweight aluminum. It can be used as a proper fork for light digging, as a rake to gather dead leaves and generally tidy up, to pull down climbers requiring pruning, and as an all-purpose soil scarifier and aerator.

You will also need a pair of pruning shears; buy good-quality ones and make sure they have a notch for cutting wire as this will prevent your blades being ruined. A two-handled lopper is a more substantial pruner, which you may need if you have trees or older, tougher shrubs. You will only need a long-handled tree pruner, which is extendable to a good length, if you have an established container garden with tall trees and climbers.

Depending on the scale of your contained garden, there are other items of equipment that may prove useful. A polyethylene sheet with carrying handles, widely available in garden centers and mail order catalogs, can be used to empty pots onto when transplanting, as well as to mix up compost, to carry plants in or remove dead ones, and to prune directly onto when you are clearing out and cutting back. Rolls of trash bags are useful, indeed indispensable in a city garden: it is a good idea to remove all dead plants, prunings and spent soil immediately.

Other items of equipment that you will probably need at one stage or another include wall nails, vine eyes, galvanized wire and plastic-coated wire, tree and shrub ties, a hammer, bamboo of various thicknesses for stakes, an apron with pockets and assorted gloves. I personally find a builder's bucket invaluable—not only do I carry around in it all my tools, spare rolls of wire, fertilizers and other gardening paraphernalia, but it also acts as a seat when I get tired or want to prune at waist level. Brushes, long and short, and a dustpan will enable you to keep a contained garden looking pristine.

TOOLS AND EQUIPMENT

Watering can
  (with detachable rose)

Hand trowel

Hand fork

Long-handled fork

Dibble

Pruning shears with
  brightly colored handles

Polyethylene sheet with
  carrying handles

Gardening apron

Gardening gloves

Wire, ties and string

Rolls of trash bags

Bamboo stakes

Dustpan and brush

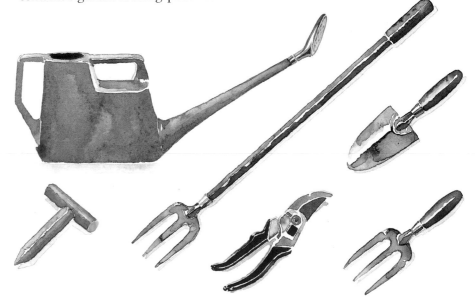

Watering and feeding

Plants confined to a limited space require far more care and pampering than their free friends. Trees, shrubs and bedding plants in a garden border can always extend their roots further down in the soil during a dry spell or for extra nutrients. But container-grown subjects are entirely at our mercy and need a regular supply of water and food, since rain often fails to penetrate a densely planted pot and the nutrients in potting compost are soon used up.

Watering your contained garden

Well-filled containers can dry out surprisingly quickly, even in damp winter weather, while on a sunny terrace in summer twice-daily watering is sometimes needed. Water early in the morning and again, if necessary, in the evening during summer; do not water in the heat of the day. In winter, water in late morning whenever it is needed, and only when no frost threatens. Experience is the best teacher about when, and how much, to water: put your finger into a pot and feel the soil at least 4 in. down, remembering how crowded and cramped the plant's roots soon become. You can force a pointed bamboo stick down a crowded pot to allow water to penetrate better.

Container watering must be done gently and thoroughly. The best way is to go from one pot to another with a slow-running hose, only stopping when you see water coming out of the bottom. The more time-consuming alternative is to use a watering can and water through the rose. On a dry terrace, some plants—particularly evergreens and conifers —benefit from a thorough spraying carried out in the cool of the evening.

Special devices are available for high-level watering, such as hanging baskets. You can have your basket on pulley hangers which can be raised or lowered as required, or use the special long-arm attachment for cans. These can be fixed to a carrying device slung over your arm and manipulated all around a terrace.

Sometimes, despite all your efforts, a pot dries out completely, leaving its occupants drooping sadly, huddled miseries en route to the grave. They may occasionally revive with frequent, very careful soaking, combined with overhead spraying, a spell in the shade, and judicious cutting back of frizzled branches. Do not cast out the pot's subjects until some weeks have passed, in case a tree or shrub may start to sprout from the pruned area, or a bedding plant from the base.

Anyone with wandering intentions and a shortage of handy friends should investigate self-watering systems. These come in many guises, from computer-controlled state-of-the-art feats of engineering to pieces of string sitting in a bucket of water reaching to your pots. The simplest ready-made system consists of a hose with small tubes running to each pot, through which a small amount of water trickles; this is fairly foolproof provided the outlets are kept clear. Trays covered with water-retentive granules or capillary matting can hold several pots and this will suffice for a short vacation period. A covering of bark or peat-substitute also helps to keep evaporation down.

If you are embarking on raised beds, it would be sensible to build in the best self-watering system available. Most modern nurseries have been forced to install some device and many specialist gardening magazines advise and instruct in this field. The computer-controlled systems also supply liquid fertilizer and make maintenance of the container garden considerably easier. Nothing equals an experienced owner inspecting the pots regularly, of course, but where there are a lot of containers, attempts to streamline the process should be encouraged.

Feeding your plants

One of the ironies of gardening is that we continually feed and stimulate the growth of plants which we then spend long hours cutting back; but the point is that healthy growth and happy plants look infinitely better than miserable, half-starved little objects that never grow. If you have filled your containers with a brand-name soil-based compost, it will contain slow-release, balanced nutrients which provide your plants with a good start. However, watering will soon cause these to leach out and you will then need to supplement the nutrients by giving your plants regular feeds.

***Origanum*
'Kent Beauty'**
This engaging cultivar of Origanum rotundifolium *has aromatic, round-oval, blue-green leaves that trail elegantly over the edge of a low bowl and produces masses of delicate pale pink flowers with mauve bracts all summer. The species was used by monks in herbariums from the thirteenth century onward for its medicinal properties. Oil extracted from its stems was used to dull the pain of toothache, infusions of the flowers were headache cures and the dried leaves were applied as compresses to soothe pain or swelling.*

Find a good general fertilizer, high in nitrogen, and preferably one that is designed for all soil types, acid or alkaline, that can be used both as a normal feed and as a foliar feed. A seaweed-based fertilizer is fine, provided you do not object to your garden smelling of the seashore for a few hours. Another good choice is one that resembles a liquid manure. An additional advantage of this is that it contains a good proportion of nitrogen and will also come in handy for the instant aging of stone or concrete if painted on the outside of pots.

I water permanent plantings with a diluted mixture of a liquid plant feed at least once a month in the growing season, using an additional foliar feed on recalcitrant plantings when they need it. But annuals and temporary bedding plants need a weekly feed during the summer months, at the height of the flowering season. I generally favor a cocktail approach, using one brand for several weeks, then another for a change. In addition, twice a year I apply a brand-name tonic containing iron chelate, magnesium and manganese to all camellias, pieris, rhododendrons, azaleas and other plants that prefer acidic compost. I give roses a generous specific rose fertilizer when planted, and top-up dressings in early spring, mid-summer and late summer. Read the label carefully before applying any of these treatments—the correct dosage is carefully worked out by experts and should not be exceeded.

Among the plethora of gardening aids are nutrient sticks, which contain slow-releasing fertilizers and are designed specifically for feeding plants in pots. They are particularly useful for a window box that is difficult to reach or an awkwardly placed hanging basket. As with all feeds, it is important to read and follow the manufacturer's instructions.

Besides the regular foliar and liquid feeding, with long-staying occupants it is important to top-dress (see below) and replace topsoil where possible, at least once a year, because the restrictions imposed on plants by containers must be counterbalanced by generosity in other directions. In addition, every time you add new bedding plants to a permanent planting—for instance, where there is a space designated for seasonal planting among shrubs—work in a few handfuls of compost first. If you have a large raised bed with mixed occupants, put a few handfuls of general-purpose fertilizer or granular compound into each planting hole.

With smaller containers, or those intended for bedding plants only, it is better to empty the old soil out completely (spread it over the garden if you have one), then replant using fresh compost or acidic soil. The problems arise when you have, say, lilies in a pot which you do not wish to disturb, and you intend putting new bedding on top. In such cases, remove as much compost as possible, without disturbing any bulbs, and replace with new.

TOP-DRESSING RECIPES

- If you have access to home-made compost, use this as your basis.
- Add a little blood and bone, or blood, fish and bone, and perhaps some peat-substitute, to make a well-mixed "pudding."
- When compost is not available, use one of the brand-name top-dressings sold in garden centers.
- A blend of peat-substitute or organic matter, seaweed and plant foods will be easy to handle and very effective.
- I always top-dress hosta-filled containers with solid handfuls of well-rotted manure, or a ready-made compound.
- Mushroom compost is excellent for all except acid-loving subjects.

Top-dressing

Each spring, check your permanent plantings and try to remove at least some of the top layer of soil, digging down the sides of a pot and gently scraping away as much soil as you can manage. Sometimes it helps to turn a pot sideways and roll it around a little and poke down the sides with a sharp stick.

Work the top-dressing (see recipes above) into your pot, poking a few holes into the root mass. Give the pot a good shaking and then a thorough watering before covering the top with a thin layer of brand-name compost.

Use a bamboo stick to help loosen and aerate some of the compacted soil further down (left).

Once you have added fresh compost to the pot with a trowel (right), firm it down with your fingers to get rid of any air pockets.

General upkeep

The everyday management of a container garden comes under the category of "outdoor housework," an assemblage of routine tasks designed to keep your plants looking their best for as long as possible. Dead-heading, while not the most creative aspect of container gardening, is imperative if you intend anything which flowers to continue to do so. Supporting larger plants stops them flopping forward and smothering more delicate subjects. The upkeep of a container garden also inevitably includes re-potting, since all healthy permanent plants eventually outgrow their containers.

If you are growing a climber in a free-standing pot, insert a sturdy trellis against which to train it.

Dead-heading

Removing spent and faded flowers prevents bedding plants producing seeds, thus weakening the plant. If such plants are regularly dead-headed, this prolongs the flowering season and prevents them looking untidy. The art of dead-heading lies in doing it often enough, and doing it correctly. Over-enthusiastic flower removal could result in nothing but buds surrounded by foliage. If possible, make a daily trip to the flowering annuals or mixed plantings, and remove every fading pansy, petunia and pelargonium to ensure a long flowering life.

Certain plants require particular attention in this regard. With *Argyranthemum frutescens*, for example, each flower that looks even faintly off-color should be cut off by tracing its joint right back to the beginnings of another bud. This delight of summer will flower until the first frosts if treated correctly.

If you intend going away for longer than a few days, consider cutting off all the flowers on many of the plants in the enclosed garden: all roses in full flower, hebes, verbenas, violas, sweet peas, daisy bushes, gazanias, felicias, arctotis and polyanthus. You leave a garden bereft, but return to one full of flowers, which is preferable to lots of dead roses.

Support and staking

Most climbers from a nursery are sold complete with a bamboo stake to which your plant is attached—loosen it if it is too restrictive, but leave it firmly wedded to this (or a stouter one if need be), should there be a gap between your container and the wall. A tall shrub when placed against a wall will generally try to lean forward for better light and needs a restraining stake to keep it upright. Insert quite a short one into the middle of its foliage, thus forcing it back.

Tying in of climbers is as important as pruning (see page 32), of which it becomes a part. The aim is to allow your climbers to spread only where you wish them to; if you have put in trellis or wires and planned their route wisely, you can allow them straying space but not total freedom.

Potting Plants

Place the two pots, old and new, side by side on a polyethylene sheet, and prepare the new one with a liner, drainage material and a good layer of new soil before starting to do battle with the old one. Once the plant is out of its old pot, shake the compacted rootball in order to dislodge some soil. Lift the plant into the prepared new container, firming new soil all around the roots as you go. Cut back any broken or damaged leaves and branches, then water the pot copiously and spray the foliage.

If you wish to replace the pot with a larger one, keeping the same plants, remove some of the older roots and any drainage material from the base.

Jiggle the pot to shake the soil down or use a stick to push the soil down around the edges.

Repotting

Spring is the favored time for a complete overhaul of your container-grown permanent plants. Inspect all pots apart from those for spring interest, and look for a chance to improve them. Anything obviously bursting out of its pot but manageable enough to deserve a larger one is a prime candidate. Find a larger replacement pot—taking both depth and girth into account and ensuring room for drainage as well as more soil. For smaller plants, the general principle is not to use too large a replacement pot—ideally an additional 3–6 in. all round.

If the shrub is small and its home round, loosening the soil all around the edges with a trowel or old kitchen knife may suffice and the plant may come out as from a grower's pot. If it is large and has been in its present container for some time, sharing it with other plants, your task is more difficult and you will need help. Even quite large containers can be safely turned on their sides, with one person holding the pot and another the plant. Terra-cotta responds to being rolled to and fro, after the loosening process (it helps to wrap the tree or shrub in a sheet first to protect it while rolling). If you can manage to tip the container sideways, but not flat on the ground, this is better for the plant but very much harder for the poor pot-supporter.

When the plants are newly installed in their bigger pot, as explained opposite, try to leave the entire container in the shade for some days, spraying frequently, and hoping for rain. Do not despair if the plants wilt; they might well do so after the shock of being moved, but they usually recover within a month or so and start growing again.

Rescue

For those whose container planting is part of a larger garden, it is reassuring to know that a precious tree or shrub that has outgrown even the largest pot can be removed from its container and put out to grass, to enjoy a more dignified middle life in a garden bed. Almost any plant that has been in a confined space will transplant happily into open ground, and respond to its new freedom with glee, growing vigorously as if to make up for lost time. Most bulbs, too, given a year to recover, will flower and multiply

happily in a garden. If you have space in a garden you can decide to replant and replace ailing trees and shrubs where necessary, without suffering pangs of conscience. For example, roses grown in good-sized tubs or troughs may do well for some three or four years, but after that often deteriorate or begin to suffer from die-back. In raised beds, which provide a far larger root run, they may flourish for as long as seven years. But even this is a short time in gardening and you would be happier planting roses in containers in the knowledge that they could be transplanted into a larger border when they cease to thrive. For those whose only garden is in containers, this may mean finding a friend with a large and welcoming country garden who will gladly accept fugitives from restricted city homes.

The size of this pot is adequate for a well-grown shrub, such as this lacecap hydrangea, for several years, provided it is top-dressed with fresh compost every spring. When the shrub eventually outgrows its container it will have to be planted, into a bigger one, or removed to a border in the garden where it can grow freely.

Pruning

There are several reasons for pruning trees and shrubs. Foremost, in the delightful phrase of gardening writer Christopher Lloyd, is "girth control": large, healthy plants confined to a small space inevitably need controlling. In a solely contained garden, scale must be maintained by judicious removal of parts of one plant to allow a follow-on planting to get established. Certain plants, such as roses, some shrubs and many climbers, require pruning in order to flower properly. Plant health also plays a part—the natural dying back of a limb, through accident or disease, needs to be accelerated to prevent rotting wood or leaves collecting.

Accurate and detailed pruning instructions for all types of plant are to be found in books dedicated to the subject. More general guidelines are given here for our purposes. The illustrations show the correct way to make a pruning cut, and advice on when and how much to prune is given below, grouped by species. It is worth getting to know your shrubs' habits and how they refurbish themselves.

It is good practice always to keep a pair of pruning shears handy when you go around your container garden, to snip off untidy bits, too invasive tendrils or unwieldy branches. Remove all prunings as soon as possible: nothing looks less alluring than a smelly pile of dead branches stuffed in a corner, breeding pests. If you have a shrub whose attractive foliage you might use in the house, such as a pittosporum, a hebe, a ceanothus or a *Viburnum tinus*, cut it regularly to ensure that the plant looks balanced.

Trees Most trees that you are likely to try and grow in a container can be pruned, such as *Robinia pseudoacacia* 'Frisia,' whose brilliant golden leaves would otherwise threaten to darken your rooms, the *Eucalyptus gunnii* waving silvery leaves increasingly far above you, and the *Acer negundo* 'Flamingo' spreading toward your neighbor. Use the long-handled pruner for tall trees; ideally, work with a partner who can direct your wavering arm.

When pruning trees, try to choose a junction at which to cut; if you are removing a branch from the main trunk, cut as near as possible to where it joins the trunk. Modern horticultural thinking has dismissed the practice of painting over a pruning cut but the principle of reward after punishment still stands: prune, then feed, is my motto.

Shrubs A large number of shrubs take cutting back and reshaping well, springing up and refurbishing themselves during a season, and these are ideally suited to growing in a container. They are listed on this page. Many willows (*Salix*), buddlejas, caryopteris and heathers insist upon severe cutting back at least in alternate years.

SHRUBS THAT RESPOND TO SEVERE PRUNING

Acacia

Berberis (many)

Brachyglottis

Buddleja

Buxus (box)

Choisya ternata (Mexican orange blossom)

Daphne odora

Eucalyptus

Euonymus

Hebe (most)

Hypericum

Ilex (holly)

Mahonia

Olearia

Piptanthus laburnifolius

Pittosporum tobira

Rhododendron

Sambucus

Santolina

Sarcococca

Viburnum (most)

Weigela

Making the correct cut

Pruning must be done sensitively and with thought for the overall shape of both plant and garden. Never lop a branch off in the middle of its growth, leaving a stump leading nowhere; either remove the branch completely or cut it back to a leaf joint or junction point as shown here. Make sure your pruning shears are sharp and clean: never hack it or tear the bark. Cut at an angle, sloping away from the leaf joint (as shown, right), so that rain does not cause the cut end to rot.

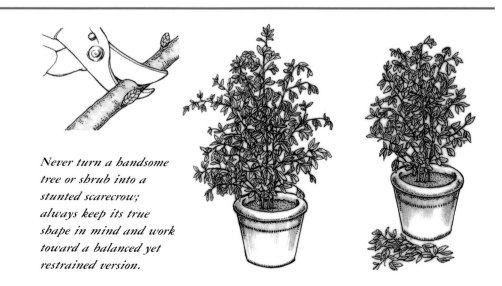

Never turn a handsome tree or shrub into a stunted scarecrow; always keep its true shape in mind and work toward a balanced yet restrained version.

Pruning is necessary to neaten and restrict the growth of trees and shrubs in containers. A judiciously pruned shrub will reward you with a pleasing overall shape and a mass of flowers, like this Choisya ternata.

branches and will obligingly produce fresh growth from quite elderly wood. They are prime examples for shapely pruning: shorten long growth back to a junction and remove weak or awkward branches entirely. Hydrangeas can be shortened back to a pair of buds or whole branches removed in late spring.

Climbers Climbers such as early-flowering *Clematis alpina*, *C. macropetala* and *C. armandii* can be cut well back as soon as the flowers begin to fade. The evergreen *Clematis armandii*, when established, benefits from ruthless removal of almost all the old stems, being given a good feed, and the new growth tied in.

Vigorous climbers will be restricted when container-grown, but will still require constant vigilance; such climbers include *Passiflora* (passion flower), *Vitis coignetiae*, *Actinida chinensis*, *Humulus* (hops), *Jasminum* (jasmines), *Solanum crispum*, *Fallopia baldschuanica* (Russian vine) and *Wisteria*.

If you have a raised bed against a trellis or a wall, with shrubs in front of climbers, never turn your back for longer than a month since such neglect will entail invasive tendril-forming climbers getting the upper hand. If this fate does befall your shrubs, the best remedy is first to cut all twining arms away from the shrubs, then to use the garden shears to cut back the offender ruthlessly. Remove enough growth to allow you to reach the trellis, and tie the climber firmly to it with twine or plastic-coated wire. Once in control you can differentiate between old and new growth, removing the former and tying in the latter.

Trailers Trailing plants such as ivy, put in to soften the edges of an urn, need to be pruned regularly. Remove old growths entirely when they have become too woody, and shorten any trailing growths which look too drawn out. Flowering trailers such as helianthemums, trailing pelargoniums, aubrietas and nepetas all need occasional nipping back to keep them bushy. *Vinca* (periwinkle), when used in mixed plantings, is best cut right back after flowering, and again in autumn, to encourage the fresh growth in spring. Silver foliage plants, such as artemisias, santolinas, helichrysums and *Brachyglottis greyi* can be pruned in spring, but are best left until cold winds and late frosts have retreated.

Some shrubs resent cuts in old wood, so you must start pruning the new growth early on: these include lavender, rosemary, cistus, genista, rue and *Cytisus battandieri*.

As a very rough guide, prune flowering shrubs directly after they have flowered. Plants which flower more or less continuously, such as some roses or *Fremontodendron californicum*, need to be cut back at intervals during the season. Camellias which begin to outgrow their space should be cut back well after their flowering; they do not mind losing whole

Training and topiary

The artificiality of container gardening has a particular affinity with topiary in all its forms. Nothing looks more elegant than a standard or half-standard in the right container, and a cluster of well-shaped box sculptures in handsome pots makes the most distinctive of container gardens. However, if you walk into a nursery and ask for a standard of almost anything, you will be shocked at the price. Training costs money—be it of doctors, ballet dancers or plants—and the main reason is the time it takes, along with the patience, discipline and attention to detail involved. But if you have the time and the patience there is no reason why you cannot be your own topiarist, and train the plants into shape yourself. For all those who want an instant garden, there are others who enjoy nibbling away at a seedling bay, found in a friend's garden, and turning it into a splendid lollipop shape on a twisted stem.

Almost any shrub or perennial with a woody stem can be turned into a standard, and the best candidates include hollies, myrtles, scented geraniums, daisy bushes, heliotropes, fuchsias and hibiscus—as well as trees such as some conifers, Japanese maples, pomegranates, orange and lemon trees. Many containerized evergreens can be clipped to form a standard—the ubiquitous hedging *Chamaecyparis*, for example, responds to the removal of its lower branches and light clipping of the remaining foliage, even when the plant is quite mature.

Training and topiary might seem synonymous; in many ways they are. You cannot create topiary until you have trained, as you cannot teach until you have tamed. You may purchase a large, shapeless box (*Buxus*) and decide to turn it into a corkscrew, but generally speaking, if you decide to embark on topiary, you will most probably search out suitable young plants, train them on and let them branch out into miraculous shapes when your plant material has grown larger. If you have time, enthusiasm and a modicum of space, try creating standards and half-standards of different types and heights. You can also create twisted stems, by winding the young stem around a stake (as shown on page 81). *Wisteria sinensis* 'Black Dragon' makes a spectacular feature as a twisted-stem standard in an enormous pot.

The variations on the theme of topiary are legion. You can create shapes of ball, pyramid, corkscrew, bird, animal or fantasy. Just as sculptors see their finished work within a block of marble, you can let a box grow as it will at the outset, feeding and turning it regularly, and decide on its shape—be it animal or geometric—as something begins to emerge. You can also make false topiary of plants such as ivy, by fixing a soil-filled pot inside a wire globe attached to a stout stem, training the ivy out and around the globe as shown below. Ivy lends itself happily to these "faux"

(as shown on page 81)

TREES AND SHRUBS FOR TOPIARY

Buxus koreana

Buxus sempervirens 'Elegantissima' and 'Gold Tip'

Caragana arborescens

Cotoneaster (many cultivars)

Elaeagnus

Euonymus fortunei 'Silver Pillar' and 'Silver 'n' Gold'

Forsythia

Genista

Kochia scoparia trichophylla (tender, but fast-growing)

Laurus nobilis (sweet bay)

Ligustrum (privet)

Prunus lusitanica (Portuguese laurel)

Prunus pissardii

Prunus subhirtella

Rhamnus alaternus

Viburnum (smaller cultivars)

Training a standard

The basic principle is to tie the main stem of an upright-growing or weeping plant to a stake, remove all the lower growths and allow the top gradually to form a particular shape, trimming to encourage and maintain it. Throughout, feed the plant with general fertilizer and foliar feeds.

A tree with a naturally weeping habit should only be allowed to follow its own bent once it reaches the desired height. It will require careful thinning out and shortening of the branches to maintain its line.

Tie the main stem of a juvenile evergreen shrub firmly to a stake.

Remove all the emergent shoots from the lower part of the main stem.

Clip the underside flat, once it is well grown, to form a solid mophead.

topiary games, and the results can brighten a winter container immeasurably, particularly when a brightly variegated cultivar is used. *Hedera* 'Goldheart,' though slow-growing, is charming, cheerful and very amenable.

Never take any shortcuts with the care and maintenance of trained subjects and topiary: just a brief spot of neglect can ruin years of dedicated pampering. An elegant twisted box corkscrew will simply die if left unwatered for a vacation period. Standards tend to be more delicate than the same plant growing freely; they therefore require more shelter and protection from wind and frost. A cool greenhouse, or a short spell indoors, is sometimes necessary in the cold winter months; failing this, you might need to make a "winter overcoat" as described on page 37. Standards also require turning frequently, to allow light to reach all sides evenly. Remember to repot the mature plants from time to time (see page 31).

The pruning of standard and topiary trees and bushes, once established, is a matter of keeping them trim and not allowing them to lose their hard-won shape. Sweet bay, in particular, needs trimming and feeding in late spring, and most probably spraying with a pest destroyer too, since they are martyrs to infestation. Standard conifers, such as *Cupressus glabra* or *Juniperus × media* 'Pfitzeriana Aurea,' will need inspecting for browning foliage within the

False topiary

To create a "standard" of pot-grown ivy, fix a substantial pot on top of a stake using brackets or metal cross-pieces. Surround this with a circular cage of heavy-duty wire, and train the plant's stems around the globe, eventually to cover it. Fix the upright in a decorative pot filled with gravel and cover it with sphagnum moss. This method could also be used for early-flowering summer jasmine or passion flower. They would all need plenty of watering and feeding, and must never be allowed to dry out.

A group of topiary box (Buxus sempervirens) in pots forms a handsome collection. Any of this small group of clipped box can be deployed where needed to act as sentinels at the edge of a path or lawn, or to add an air of permanence to a summer composition.

head; this should be cut out, with any dead branchlets. Standard weeping cotoneasters and small weeping trees, such as *Salix caprea* 'Pendula,' must be pruned from within, retaining the bell shape on which they are based, to prevent them becoming a twisted and tangled mess.

Protecting containers

The protection of your container-grown plants involves sheltering them from the worst of the elements, chiefly frost and cold winds. It also means protecting them from assault by garden pests and diseases, which is as much to do with buying resistant cultivars as with regular inspection.

Winter protection

If frost penetrates the roots of a container-grown plant, it threatens both plant and container. In the past, precious urns were wrapped in straw-filled burlap when they were too large to bring into a sheltered orangery. Protecting containers in the winter is now less of a problem than it used to be, since most modern containers are sold as frost-proof; however, this of course depends on the degree of cold and how exposed the situation is, and frost-proofing cannot be unconditionally guaranteed.

In towns, the buildings create additional warmth, and delicate plants in urban containers have a greater chance of survival than those in the open. It is easier to spread a thick layer of bark chippings over something tender in a pot than it is over half an acre of windswept garden in the country. Provided you have ensured good drainage, and there is no pool of water trapped in the base to freeze and crack your pot, most city containers and their plants survive well. If trees and shrubs are kept on the dry side during winter, this further improves their chances. Where possible, huddle containers together to help protect each other, rather than leaving them alone and thus even more exposed.

Any delicate, semi-tender plants should, ideally, have a backup of cuttings (see page 39) that can be kept protected to substitute for any plants that you may lose. Failing all this, be philosophical, and regard a loss as a challenge.

Steps should be taken to protect the semi-tender Cordyline australis *at the first sign of frost. It needs extra well-draining compost, with plenty of grit mixed in and a thick layer of drainage material at the base of the pot. It is best positioned in a sheltered corner of the garden, out of the line of east and north winds.*

Protection against pests and diseases

It is always amazing how short a time it takes the usual garden menaces to discover your single plant in a pot before it has even been turned into a contained garden. Aphids and whitefly seem to arrive, singly or together, within hours of planting. It is important not to make matters worse by bringing in plants already infested, whether from a nursery or garden center, so inspect with vigilance any plants you intend to buy. In early spring some growers produce shrubs from a growing tunnel whose soft foliage has not been sufficiently hardened and they may harbor the dreaded red spider mite so prevalent in under-glass propagation.

Everyone has to formulate his own approach to pests, but most of us would prefer not to use a mass of chemicals and to stick, if possible, to a reasonably sound ecological method of control. Because a contained garden is generally smaller than an open one, and more easily inspected, actually removing pests by hand becomes an option. Besides using your eyes and hands, another good weapon is the hose—a blast from it will often wash away a good many invaders, once spotted, as will a wipe over large leaves with a damp cloth. There are now a good many organic remedies for various ills and I would advise using these lightly and only resorting to chemical weapons when desperate. The only exception I make is in spraying my roses with a brand-name all-purpose anti-mildew, black spot and aphid compound according to the manufacturer's instructions. Before planting any roses, check their record, since some cultivars are particularly disease-resistant while others are martyrs to mildew and black spot.

The organic solution to aphids has always been to encourage ladybugs, their natural predators, to do their job by placing any you may find directly onto infested leaves. Small birds are excellent aphid warriors too; the shrubs on which they perch remain trouble-free, so try hanging your winter bird-feeder near any roses or camellias to enlist their help. Caterpillars are easily spotted and can be removed by hand, as are snails and slugs—gardeners have to be brave and unsqueamish about pests.

Hygiene, that staple of good management, is of paramount importance in container gardening and should be rigorously observed. The daily trip to inspect and dead-head your plants should include the removal of all dead or dying foliage, indeed anything which looks unhealthy—remember that a leaf turning yellow is never going to turn back to green. Remove it, and never leave dead stems, rotting flowers or unhealthy-looking plants to infect the rest. It is vital to sweep your terrace, roof or balcony regularly, since a buildup of leaves soon offers a haven for something undesirable. After sweeping and clearing all the debris away, hose down both plants and paving.

Protection against frost

It is certainly worth taking precautions to protect tender subjects against frost damage during a cold winter. The plastic bubble-wrap used to protect china and pictures makes good insulation for container-grown plants —it can be wrapped around a delicate species in winter and tied in place with string. Another idea is to form some nylon mesh into a wigwam with bamboo canes, and place it around a pot whose occupant might succumb to severe frost.

A winter overcoat can be made from a sandwich of chicken wire filled with bracken fern and wrapped around a container (left).

Spreading plants such as cordylines can have their spikes tied together, to provide a degree of protection (right).

Raising your own plants

Whether you are inspired by motives of thrift, or the sense of power or the touch of magic, there is no doubt about the pleasure to be derived from growing your own plants from seeds and cuttings. The cuttings or bits of plants may be presents from friends, which give them a special significance. Raising plants from seed involves all the studying, waiting, and the thrill of seeing the amazingly defined character of even minute seedlings. Such propagation allows you to choose unusual plants, to surprise yourself and impress visitors, and provides one of gardening's most satisfying experiences. Standing under a spreading tree you have grown from a seed makes you truly part of a special tribe.

Growing from seed

Growing any plant from seed is tremendous fun—even experienced gardeners respond to the first bumps on the compost and enjoy watching the first leaves forming on the seedlings. If you have a regular garden, with the normal amount of space for planting, potting and maybe even a greenhouse or frame, you can enjoy this most satisfying aspect of horticulture. However, when dealing with container gardens exclusively—if you possess only a postage-stamp space, or are struggling to create an oasis within your windy city roof—it is admittedly more difficult to find the necessary space.

The most easily grown plants for containers will be annuals, hardy and half-hardy, whose quickly achieved maturity allows them to flower over a season without requiring over-wintering space. Decide what you feel like experimenting with, buy some seed compost, and get hold of seed trays, pieces of glass, drainage material and spare small flowerpots. Annual climbers, such as morning glory, climbing nasturtiums, *Cobaea scandens*, sweet peas, or runner beans can be started off in a smallish pot. (Refrain from putting your morning glories outside until the nights warm up a little, since too chilly a night checks them and browns their leaves.) If you have spare containers and space, you can sow easy annuals, such as alyssum, trailing nasturtiums, marigolds, pansies, violas, nemophilas, stocks, cosmos, antirrhinums or anything else which lures you from its packet.

Many annuals will in fact sow themselves in your window box, so learn to recognize seedlings of all types so that you do not pull them up as weeds. Lobelias are particularly obliging, as are ageratum and nasturtiums; baby pansies and lupins have particular charm, and the swords of *Sisyrinchium*

Sowing seeds

Place the drainage material in your tray or pot and cover it with seed compost. Water well and scatter your seeds on top, covering them lightly, according to the instructions on the packet. Lay a piece of glass on top, raised slightly for air circulation, and cover with a sheet of newspaper. Remove these at the first sight of a seedling. Check that the compost is always moist, and water gently through a fine rose. If your trays are out of doors, keep the young seedlings in part-shade; if inside, make sure they never dry out.

When the seedlings are big enough to handle, use a plant label to transplant them into a larger tray or container.

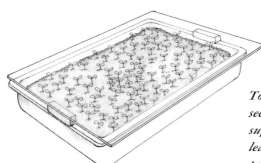

To sow annual climbers, place three or four seeds into a 7 in. pot with fine sticks to support them. Remove the weaker ones to leave two plants; insert these into a larger pot when they are about 16 in. high.

come like a wolf on the fold. *Helleborus foetidus* has a delightful habit of producing its babies, dark green shiny hands, fresh and full of life, in most unexpected nooks, and frequently presents you with a full-sized plant about to open its green flowers. *Erigeron mucronatus* sows itself with the utmost profligacy in every corner, covering paving with its neat, cheerful miniature daisies.

If space restricts you from raising seeds, some garden centers and growers produce small plantlets of various desirable container species—pelargoniums, petunias, fuchsias or climbers—ready for transplanting. It can be fun to watch these grow, and they are particularly suitable for tucking into your hanging baskets.

Taking cuttings

Cuttings are an excellent way of increasing your choice of container material. Always keep a large, shallow terra-cotta bowl tucked in a shady corner and filled with cuttings compost, ready to receive any offerings you get from friends. It is deeply satisfying to produce a flourishing shrub or plant from one little cutting, and more so when it has some association with a friend, or has been donated by a fellow enthusiast. Generosity among gardeners is

endemic, so it is also nice to have some spares to hand out oneself.

Suitable shrubby candidates for propagating from cuttings includes hebes, fuchsias, pelargoniums, *Impatiens*, lavender, lavatera, Daphnes, skimmias and ceanothus. Most of the semi-hardy material so useful for containers can also be propagated by cuttings, kept in a frost-free place in winter: felicias, helichrysums, cineraria, salvias, osteospermums, gazanias, argyranthemums.

At almost any time during the growing season you can cut off pieces of ornamental-leaved pelargonium (such as *P.* 'Lady Plymouth,' *P. crispus*, *P. tomentosum*) and push them into a pot, where they will grow happily. When cutting back fuchsias in late spring, it is worth putting the twiggy prunings into a spare corner, particularly those of *Fuchsia magellanica* cultivars. The larger-flowered fuchsias will generally produce roots when placed in a glass jar filled with water, as will *Impatiens* and the ubiquitous spider plant, *Chlorophytum variegatum*, itself a splendid hanging basket or pot dweller. Simply set a piece of cardboard on the jar, making holes to keep your cuttings upright and separate, and leave it on a kitchen windowsill. This appeals greatly to children and is a good way to start them off (see page 94).

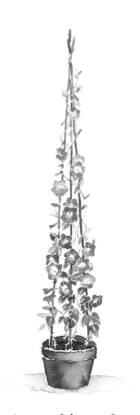

A successful way of growing annual climbers such as morning glory, French beans or sweet peas is to train them up three bamboo sticks.

Taking stem cuttings

This method of propagation is suitable for most half-hardy bedding plants as well as some shrubby species. Sever a non-flowering shoot with a sharp knife where a leaf joins the stem, and remove the lower leaves. Dip the cutting into a hormone rooting powder, and insert it firmly into a pot filled with gritty compost. Make a primitive "greenhouse" with a polyethylene bag, and keep an eye on its occupants. Resist the temptation to remove cuttings until visible growth and tug-resisting roots are manifest.

Cut off a healthy shoot using pruning shears or a sharp knife.

Dust the cut end with hormone rooting powder to encourage roots to form quickly.

Insert three or four cuttings into an 8 in. pot filled with compost to which some grit has been added.

CONTAINERS FOR ALL SITUATIONS

There are as many ways of using containers as there are styles of gardening. In some cases, there is no alternative to using containers because space and the building preclude all other forms of gardening. This is especially true of city apartments, with their roof gardens and balconies, and small town houses, many of which have only a tiny courtyard or paved terrace at the back and space for a couple of window boxes at the front. But container gardening is not the sole prerogative of city dwellers, nor does necessity alone dictate its use.

Large pots of well-grown Hydrangea macrophylla *'Madame Emile Mouillère' set against a shady wall, the pink and white theme echoed by* Abelia grandiflora *in the left foreground. Use of a single plant with good shape and long-lasting flowers suited to shade has more impact in such situations than mixed plantings.*

Containers within a garden

The bold simplicity of this pair of handsome stone pots planted with matching variegated yuccas illustrates the impact that well-placed containers can provide in a large garden. Here they act as living statues, drawing the eye through the arch in the high hedge to what lies beyond, and creating a magnificent focal point.

The background of plant material within a garden often provides the right degree of contrast to offset planting within a container. Traditionally, containers have always been used to enhance the very largest and grandest gardens, and this gives us the chance to study the plants at their best, both because of the spacious background and the wide choice of classical urns or planters and plant material that is available.

Many of these large, well-managed gardens on a grand scale are open to the public and, because they have greater resources than most of us have, their container plantings can teach us a great deal. Your own garden may be much more modest and without such a glorious abundance of plant material, nor any of the magnificent stone urns or lead jardinières in which to do your planting; but you can still take

inspiration from their examples: the satisfying shape of an urn on a pedestal, with plants spilling down its sides, judiciously placed to draw the eye to a marvelous view; the impact of a pair of enormous stone pots filled with color, at the top of a flight of steps; a giant oil jar pouring out a river of *Convolvulus althaeoides*, set on a raised bed underplanted with matching silver and pink; sentinels of box corkscrews marking the division between paving and grass; a superb lead cistern filled with *Helichrysum petiolare* or a copper crammed with scarlet tulips, against a dark, somber yew hedge. I do not think I have ever visited a garden of any size without learning something— even if it is what not to plant—and I generally come home with an idea for sympathetic plantings, for mixing colors, for positioning and for the vital aspect of scale.

RIGHT, TOP *The huge, glazed urn is used alone in this garden border. Its subtle shade blends well with the foliage and flowers of most plants. Light always reflects from glazed objects, and the foxgloves (Digitalis) leaning toward it show up the brilliant blue spires of* Salvia *below.*

RIGHT *A group of pots successfully softens a paved area, and this combination of formal topiary and billowing flowers creates a secret courtyard within a large garden. The tender* Bougainvillea, *trailing* Campanula *and ivies show up well against the somber evergreen topiary.*

Creating a focal point

Every garden, regardless of size, needs focal points, and well-planted urns or boxes make a splendid statement. Our eyes need to be directed to specific points to enable them to wander about comfortably in between. And a view part-glimpsed or framed gives us greater pleasure than an uninterrupted one.

A good urn on a pedestal, for example, filled with traditional pelargoniums and ivies and placed at the end of a path or under an arch, is both attractive and satisfying. The superb Ali Baba jars are a striking example of a container that can be successfully incorporated into large gardens—their comfortably rounded sides contrast well with foliage, and wherever they are placed they create interest. They would form a perfect centerpiece for an herb garden, even

left unplanted, or create a focal point in the center of a circular lawn, placed on a raised base and planted with soft trailers.

The placing of these impact-makers is important, as we have seen, and so are color and scale. An all-white planting will stand out better against a dark background, particularly in the evening, than a mixed affair. The color contrast can be more subtle, as in a bed of silver planting, with shades of blue, pink and soft mauve, in front of which stand a pair of terra-cotta pots filled with deep purple heliotrope and white petunias. A combination of perhaps two, or at the most three, colors, with appropriate foliage, is most likely to create the impact needed in a container used as a focal point. This restrained use of colors is also generally more appealing than a multi-colored planting. But to some extent this is simply a matter of taste—I have seen hanging baskets with every conceivable color and variety of annual jammed together in a haphazard fashion, looking quite splendid in their way.

Scale is a vital ingredient of all successful plantings: not only must the plants fill the container amply and harmoniously, but the whole scheme must be in scale with the setting.

Steps and boundaries

Changes of level offer great opportunities for using containers, and one of the prettiest sights in a garden is a cluster of pots marching up a handsome set of steps. There is something about the angles formed by steps that seems to demand an accent or a softening; in some cases the pots can serve a safety role, drawing attention to a change of level.

In a cottage garden, the pots can be jumbled, two or three around the bottom, a single one part way up the flight and a mixed group at the top. In more formal positions, matching stone urns add grandeur, either set on pedestals along the path leading to the steps, or standing either side of the flight. Where steps are low and wide, forming simply a change of level rather than a proper flight, pots of architectural foliage, such as *Fatsia japonica*, hostas or a cordyline, add greatly to the finished picture. Large terra-cotta pots with clipped box will mark a change of level partway along a path and protect the unwary from a tumble. Steps leading up to a doorway call out for a line of single pots with tumbling color, possibly ending in a matching pair with height and color combined. Sets of steps that lead to a sitting-out place, with a bench at the top, are made both prettier

and more enjoyable with a mass of scented plants surrounding the seat and marking the change of height.

As in all other aspects of this art, it is important to plant suitably for these step containers. Use formal planting for the matching pairs; architectural foliage for the warnings and delineators; cheerful and brightly colored flowers for the cottage effect; small, neat and trim plants for steps in a tiny courtyard. I have often admired a minute town garden that I know, which has a set of steps ending in a row of half-sized balustrades set out from the back wall by only enough to allow a line of miniature cypresses to

sit in pots, with a slightly taller pair framing the statue at the top of the steps. It is a classical landscape in miniature.

Always remember to allow room for people to climb the steps unimpeded, even after rain. Charming as it is to brush past scented foliage, soaking legs have less allure. Reserve your billowing, half-filled pathways for a corner of the garden.

Containers in a larger garden can also be used to soften a boundary line. A row of matching pots along a terrace will point to a smooth lawn. Clusters of ferns and hostas in fat bowls can nestle against a raised pond or lend shape to a paved surround.

ABOVE *The pair of basketwork terra-cotta pots, planted with white petunias, add height and importance to the pedestals on either side of the flight of steps. They turn this small garden into a stage.*

45

Cover-ups

Even in larger gardens it is often necessary to draw the eye away from something unsightly, or to hide a less than attractive bit of building. Siting a large container in the foreground to distract the viewer from a blot on the landscape is a well-known device, as is placing the right-sized pot over a manhole cover near the house. Any garden, large or small, has its working areas which are seldom of visual appeal. Garden sheds rarely match the architecture of your dwelling, but masked with trellis, climber-covered, and with a large cluster of pots and urns around them, they can disappear quite easily. While waiting for an evergreen screen to grow up, a well-filled container can distract the eye from what lies behind. In a paved garden, the "resting" area for container plantings not at their seasonal best can always be hidden by a well-grown camellia or other evergreen planted in a large pot.

Woven wooden fencing, though eminently practical and an excellent windbreak, needs disguising, and troughs of large-leaved ivies do this to perfection. Think vertically as well as laterally, and place a trough, filled with trailers, on top of an awkward wall to disguise its lack of charm.

Using pots to fill a gap

One of the main strengths of containers lies in their mobility: they can be placed in a specific location whenever they are required. If you need an instant lift for a corner of the garden lacking spice or past its seasonal best, a huge pot of lilies can be whisked into position. If you want to draw the eye past a failing border toward another vista, place a pair of brightly planted urns at the junction. A rather wintry group of evergreens can have a huge tub of early-flowering daffodils placed strategically in front of them, while a mass of petunias pouring from a pedestal will brighten a corner past its spring best.

LEFT *A large clay pot of* Zantedeschia *underplanted with trailing* Glechoma hederacea *'Variegata' becomes an important focal point in the center of this tiny, graveled courtyard with its all-white scheme.*

RIGHT *Containers can be chosen to harmonize with plants growing in a part of the garden. Here, a classic terra-cotta pot filled with tall white tulips (*Tulipa *'White Triumphator') throws the brilliant* Euphorbia *into relief and echoes the open flowers of* Magnolia *in the background.*

This ploy can be used in every aspect of container design: a pot of tulips can be dropped into the border where a gap appears; a well-clipped box shape in a handsome pot can be situated to emphasize a successful planting beside it; an etiolated shrub can hide its balding base in a froth of potted daisies; a severely pruned holly can lurk, recovering, behind a frilly fuchsia. No self-respecting container practitioner should ever be without a few top-up pots to enhance all seasons in the garden.

Growing tender plants in containers

There are other, more unusual variations on the theme of container mobility, in which tender subjects planted in containers have the benefit of being seen at their seasonal best. Bonsai trees in decorative planters can be placed outside in summer on ready-made stands at waist height; alpines in sinks or troughs (see page 98) are perfect set on a low wall, to bring their delicate charms nearer to their admirers. Provided you have a greenhouse or conservatory, or some space indoors, good-sized troughs can be planted with camellias or tender subjects ready to be taken into shelter when frost threatens. *Brugmansia cornigera* (formerly *Datura*), protected in winter and brought into a sunny courtyard in summer, makes a spectacular impact with its huge, dangling white trumpets and large, coarse leaves (see page 22). *Agapanthus* grown in low tubs or bowls look superb placed around a pool when they are in flower; their strappy leaves and upright bright blue or white flowers seem to have an affinity with the water. These are plants which particularly enjoy container life, flowering better when constricted, with their roots well baked.

If you have your own garden, a seedling or cutting can be grown on in a bed before graduating to a special position as a container-grown focal point or terrace ornament. Indeed, any self-sown seedlings that appear in your garden border can be used as part of a mixed container planting, for example those of conifers such as *Chamaecyparis lawsoniana* 'Spek' or *Thuja plicata*. It is often useful to grow such seedlings on in a good-sized plain terra-cotta pot of their own, placing the pot strategically among a group requiring evergreen balance.

Roof and balcony gardens

Roof gardens can be rather bleak, and bold planting, both of foliage and color, is needed. The golden Robinia pseudoacacia *'Frisia' and the variegated* Aucuba *will spread in their raised beds. The trailing pelargoniums bring instant summer color.*

The perimeter area of most flat roofs will usually be load-bearing, but do not forget the additional weight of wet soil and people visiting the plants, once you create a garden. The surface on which pots are to be placed has to be strong and sturdy as well as waterproof; an untreated asphalt roof would be far too soft to accept traffic and the weight of planted pots, for example. If you have containers in the middle of the roof area, try to ensure that they are being placed over a load-bearing beam or joist. Choose lightweight pots for roof gardens where possible. Drainage is also vitally important on a roof or balcony: make sure your containers drain freely and that the runoff of water can easily find an outlet that is accessible for any necessary clearing of leaves.

Roofs

If your roof is halfway up a building, with rooms below, as in some blocks of flats, and you are able to arrange a trellis around some or all of it, you are in luck. The trellis will break the wind's impact, heating from below will prevent frost damage in winter, and your roof can, indeed, become a secret garden. Always ensure that any trellis is extremely well installed: gale-force winds prowl around roof gardens even in cities, and show no mercy to flimsily erected screens.

If your roof garden is more exposed, you will have to think in terms of creating an additional windbreak with solid, hardy evergreens, such as *Ligustrum* (privet) or *Viburnum tinus*. (See the list of "Wind-Resistant Trees and Shrubs" on page 51.)

Balconies

Some balconies are also roof gardens, but a good many are entirely different and offer another set of challenges. Balconies generally serve a dual purpose, softening the building outside and providing the dweller with a retreat or additional sitting space. However, balconies are often overhung from above, preventing rain from getting to the plants, although this does offer them extra protection against the less desirable elements.

Roofs and balconies can provide a precious oasis in city life, especially when they are transformed by greenery. There is generally more scope for a roof garden, but the practical constraints may be even greater. Before placing a single pot on a roof, it is vital to ensure that the roof is both waterproof and strong enough to take the weight. Always seek the advice of an architect or builder before embarking on a new roof garden: this is doubly important when other people are involved, such as in a block of flats, or where the roof is shared.

The design of most balconies is essentially one-sided, with a flat wall or walls making a backdrop, which offers another dimension to be incorporated in your planting. You may choose to leave the walls purely as a stage against which you set your players, or you may wish to turn them into a vertical garden in their own right, with the back row of troughs or pots dedicated to climbers and wall shrubs.

One of the main ways in which a balcony differs from a roof garden is in its watering arrangements. There is rarely an outdoor tap for a balcony and, especially where there is an overhang, the plants desperately need daily watering, so attention must always be paid to the area below. Is there a drainage outlet; does it join the main drainpipe; is the surface itself waterproof? If the only watering access is via a bedroom window, for instance, consider whether you wouldn't prefer to grow a clematis or a honeysuckle up from the ground to reach the balcony and dangle over the railings, creating a balcony garden without having to struggle across the bedroom carpet carrying heavy watering cans.

This large planter, set on decking, is filled with a Rhododendron yakushimanum *and a* Brachyglottis greyi *with summer-flowering white* Impatiens. *A* Pieris *fills another pot, and* Clematis armandii *grows up with* Viburnum davidii, *adding height to the scheme.*

49

Designing the roof space

Plan out your roof garden carefully, using graph paper, as you would for any new garden before embarking on the planting. There is a wealth of difference between two or three pots plonked down next to a deckchair and a wobbling umbrella, and a properly designed space. Plan to use any available vista, whether it is the dome of a picturesque church, spreading greenery or the dramatic silhouette of high-rise apartment blocks against the skyline. Disguise wherever necessary—if there are chimneys, try and place a large pot against their supports and let something climb up them. Wind some wire loosely around the chimney pots to give a grip. *Clematis armandii* is a great evergreen cover-up, wending its elegant, spiky way around a chimney pot or unsightly drainpipe.

Decide at the planning stage what use your roof garden will have. Will you only look out on it or will you sit there in the evenings? Do you intend to spend hours sunbathing or do you hope to treat it as a real garden which happens to be on a roof? Where space, money and the building permit, an ideal roof garden should be designed for proper garden living. Some form of ornamental gazebo could be built to hold cushions and tablecloths for outdoor furniture, as well as for essential tools, fertilizers, extra compost, sprays and garden trash bags.

Containers for trees should always be an integral part of the design, as should those for permanent shrubs and mixed plantings. Extra pots for color can be added as required. If possible, allow an area for "resting" pots that can be screened by trellis or a solid evergreen. Even a small roof may offer scope for this, and it enables the visible area to look good all the time. Bulbs can be finishing their cycle, pots of lilies either coming or going, and cuttings growing on or seedlings starting, all hidden out of sight.

Choosing the plants

When a container is to hold "permanent" planting, in the form of a tree, shrub or climber, careful thought must go into your selection. The chosen species of trees, or large shrubs which can be trained as trees, as well as smaller shrubs and even bedding plants should be able to withstand the fierce winds and harsh conditions imposed by a roof. The best wind-resistant trees and shrubs are given in the list on the page opposite. Bear in mind that all soil, as well as plants and subsequent prunings, will have to be carried on and off the roof, so you cannot afford too many mistakes.

Start by using the largest practicable containers for your main plantings. Plants exposed to wind and sun dry out far more quickly than their sheltered ground-level counterparts, so the larger their root run, the greater their chance of survival. Larger pots

A sheltered rooftop

Trellis around the edges of this roof garden gives some shelter and privacy; the gazebo offers storage and a screen for resting pots. Wooden benches with lift-up lids serve as seating and storage. Lightweight, fiberglass boxes allow for seasonal change. The water garden, in a fiberglass container, should be over a load-bearing joist. The planting concentrates on foliage for year-round interest, and includes shapely trees such as *Betula pendula* (weeping silver birch) and *Malus* 'Red Jade' (crab apple).

**WIND-RESISTANT
TREES AND SHRUBS**

Acer pseudoplatanus

Ailanthus

Amelanchier

Betula

Caragana arborescens

Cotoneaster

Elaeagnus angustifolia

Forsythia

Gleditsia triacanthos

Ilex

Juniperus virginiana
  'Skyrocket'

Ligustrum lucidum

Ligustrum vulgare

Mahonia

Malus

Olearia

Pinus thunbergiana

Prunus laurocerasus

Prunus maritima

Pyracantha

Taxus baccata

Thuja orientalis

Yucca

are also more stable. One of my favorite roof gardens contains a huge Ali Baba oil jar, 4 ft. high, made in fiberglass, filled with a *Clematis armandii*, an enormous *Fatsia japonica* and a *Solanum jasminoides* 'Alba'—it dwarfs the tiny roof but gives it tremendous impact and style.

Once a pot is planted and the garden begun, maintenance comes next. Watering is vital, even in winter. You should ideally have an outside hose installed, long enough to reach all around, with an efficient drainpipe connected to the outlet from the roof, which must always be kept clear. If at all possible, install one of the simpler automatic watering systems (see page 28). Feeding and pruning are equally important to keep your roof garden looking its best all the time.

It is advisable, also, to monitor the bases of large containers on a roof, before the plants' roots begin to explore and appear through your ceiling. If the pots are raised off the floor of the roof, you can readily make sure the roots are contained, but if not, keep a careful watch. One has only to move a long undisturbed pot and see the root that has escaped through the drainage hole, coiled menacingly, awaiting its opportunity to strike, to see what I mean. This is particularly noticeable if you have covered a roof with the splendidly artificial "Astroturf" used by sports grounds. When damp, it appeals to seeds immensely—you can return from vacation to find a miniature forest sprouting merrily around the pots —though fortunately the little seedlings can be very easily uprooted.

In this rooftop oasis, planting around the sides, in troughs and various other containers, affords privacy, leaving the central area free for open-air dining.

A peaceful city retreat

For a low-maintenance sheltered roof or balcony garden that needs to look good all year round, choose a stylish but fairly hardy combination of plants. The troughs and matching square boxes used here are both decorative and substantial enough to hold several large shrubs. The inclusion of climbers trained on trellis or against walls around the circumference would create an enclosed effect.

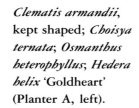

Clematis armandii, kept shaped; *Choisya ternata*; *Osmanthus heterophyllus*; *Hedera helix* 'Goldheart' (Planter A, left).

Camellia japonica 'Alba Simplex'; *Lysimachia nummularia* 'Aurea'; *Hedera helix* 'Green Ripple' (Planter B, above).

The small-leaved ivies in these planters hang down in a variegated curtain against the dark background. The only maintenance needed would be regular watering and feeding, the occasional removal of all dead foliage, and the cutting back of any over-exuberant ivy. To brighten up the whole scheme in summer, bedding plants of *Impatiens* are added to one planter and fuchsias to another, both of which flourish with scant attention, and several of the containers are underplanted with *Narcissus* 'Tête à Tête' for spring.

The square planter contains a standard *Elaeagnus* which you could trim to shape yourself (see page 34) or buy ready-trained as an expensive treat. The periwinkle (*Vinca*) should be planted to trail over the edges of the box and the violas nearer the stem of the standard shrub.

The drawing below shows how these planters could be positioned to great effect on a roof or balcony.

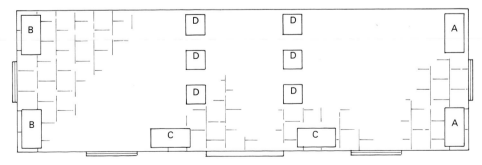

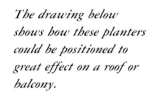

Trachelospermum jasminoides; *Rhamnus alaternus* 'Argenteovariegata,' trained to form wide pillar; *Polystichum aculeatum* 'Pulcherrimum' (Planter C, above left).

Elaeagnus pungens 'Maculata,' trained to a standard; *Vinca minor* 'Atropurpurea'; *Viola cornuta* 'Jersey Gem' (Box planter D, above).

Planning a balcony

As with a roof garden, it is important to decide exactly what you want from your balcony. If it is only to be viewed from outside, treat it as a large window box, always blending its style with that of the building. You may also want to blend the colors with the interior decorations of the room overlooking your balcony.

You might look onto an unlovely building or one whose occupants make appalling noises: air conditioning, loading of trucks, let alone parties. Some modern blocks provide quite small balconies whose retaining walls allow for good-sized troughs to be set on them. Leave the space below for sitting on and make your troughs a well-planted barrier against intrusion. Our old friend *Cordyline australis* provides a good baffle, and it could be set as a centerpiece with thick planting around it. Ensure that the troughs are well anchored, and include trailers that will grow toward your seats below. It is sometimes practicable to have two tiers of boxes or troughs in this type of balcony, in which case the lower tier would require planting for shade, whatever the aspect of the balcony.

If you can sit out on your balcony, think about scent and the time of day you might use it most before choosing your plants (see list on page 97). Bear in mind that plants set in the well formed by

An elegant shady balcony

This small balcony on a formal town house leads out from the sitting room, behind elegant wrought-iron railings. Because shaded town areas need light, white-painted boxes have been used; on the sunny side of the street, black or darkest green would be good. The standard and corkscrew-trained box need meticulous grooming, and the row of skimmias in their simple troughs would require regular feeding, but, apart from watering, this collection would be trouble-free.

some modern balconies will reach for the light, thereby turning their backs on you, so make sure you include some plants with bold shapes and, where possible, climbers to clothe the side and even hang down all around, forming a frame for the view.

Where practicable, glass or trellis screens make a valuable contribution, providing shelter for both plants and people. Some balcony owners decide to glass in part of the space, creating almost a greenhouse or conservatory. There are period buildings in cities where an internal balcony is formed in the well, and this calls for lush, romantic planting, including perhaps some of the tender camellias, and palms such as the Kentia, more usually grown indoors, and certainly the handsome Chusan palm, *Trachycarpus fortunei*. This might be a good spot for "faux" topiary (see page 34) and great pots of hydrangeas. If it happened to be light, try a tender *Ficus benjamina*, the weeping fig grown outdoors in tropical climates, which grows to a huge, superbly elegant tree when protected.

In the city, the balcony might serve only as a backdrop to curtains and never-opened windows (except for watering), in which case you might choose a simple but stylish planting scheme like a pair of standard bays in matching boxes, with a trough between containing a central *Cordyline australis* and a low hedge of *Hebe* 'Green Globe.' Standard fuchsias make good balcony plants, giving the necessary height and flowering all summer.

The balcony's aspect

Aspect plays a large part in your choice of plants. A sheltered south- or west-facing balcony could be filled with semi-tender climbers; suitable candidates include *Rhodochiton atrosanguineum*, with its delicate deep purple bells all summer and matching purple foliage; *Trachelospermum jasminoides*, with wonderfully scented white flowers; *Eccremocarpus scaber*, a vigorous evergreen with scarlet to yellow tubular flowers in late summer to autumn; *Plumbago auriculata*, with sky-blue flowers from early summer to early winter; *Berberidopsis corallina*, with deep red flowers from summer to autumn; and morning glory (*Ipomaea*), which can be grown from seed placed directly in pots, trained up a wigwam (see page 39).

A sheltered but shady balcony would offer a haven for the elegant *Acer japonicum* cultivars, where their foliage would not get blasted; they could spread gracefully and their shapely winter-bare form would look pretty against the sky.

Shapes are particularly important in winter, where a balcony is visible from your sitting room. Besides the acers, if you have space try a small weeping tree such as *Caragana arborescens*, *Salix caprea* or *Betula pendula*. The tree can be underplanted with winter-flowering pansies and small trailing ivies. Some species of privet, particularly *Ligustrum lucidum* 'Excelsum Superbum' and *Ligustrum sinense* 'Variegatum,' form delightful small branching trees, perfect in a large container; they can be underplanted with spring bulbs, followed by summer bedding.

ABOVE *The intimate atmosphere of this balcony is enhanced by the simple planting. The conical bay trees are balanced by the* Argyranthemum frutescens. *Two pot-grown mounds of* Soleirolia soleirolii *sit in between.*

OPPOSITE *On this small balcony a weeping fruit tree in a large planter co-exists with a pot-grown herb garden in miniature.*

Containers for paved areas

beautifying and adding variety to these otherwise stark outdoor spaces. Their positioning, both in relation to each other and to the whole area, should be carefully considered (see pages 60–61).

Before you embark on any planting scheme, consider whether you want an area to sit in, work in, or just to look at. If you dislike gardening and are very busy, yet want to look out on something acceptable from your study window, consider covering the entire paved area in gravel, investing in an enormous decorative urn, planting one very special tree or shrub in it, and retiring to your armchair. If you long for greenery and enjoy pottering, yet own a dank courtyard surrounded by high walls admitting very little light, do not despair. Such a courtyard can be given an imaginative treatment that will lift your spirits (see pages 58–61).

In this approach to a paved garden, the style is restrained and architectural. In a trio of matching pots, clipped box balls point to the magnificent Gunnera manicata, *more often found beside lakes.*

The term "paved area" covers everything from a setting for a single pot outside a kitchen window to broad expanses of paved garden whose lead cisterns support gnarled old trees and a forest of shrubs. It may be a yard or a courtyard, in other words a small, totally enclosed and often overlooked city garden. Or it may be a paved terrace or patio area adjoining the house, which is normally used to sit out on in summer, and which may or may not lead onto a much larger garden. In all cases, containers have an important role to play in softening as well as in

BELOW LEFT *This view through French doors reveals the author's contained garden in autumn. In total contrast to the restrained approach of the paved garden shown on the left, this illustrates the author's belief in cramming a large number of plants into the available space.* Vitis coignetiae *and* V. vinifera 'Purpurea' *mingle with* Clematis tetrarose *above eye level, while the pair of standard* Cupressus glabra *are placed either side of the pond. Foreground pots contain* Fuchsia 'Thalia,' Euonymus fortunei *and Universal Plus pansies.*

Plants for paving

All paved areas need at least one substantial container-grown plant as a focus, and among those with a long shelf life are hydrangeas, yuccas and camellias. Hydrangeas in their many forms require prodigious quantities of water but are rewarding for several months, flowering even in deepest shade. Yuccas in all varieties provide a splendid sharp contrast to softer, rounded plants, as does *Phormium tenax*, the New Zealand flax. For my taste, these look their best alone in a substantial tub, kept very well groomed and used to dominate a group of containers.

But more than any other plant, camellias in all their forms enhance courtyards and paved areas. Their almost artificial air is perfectly suited to container life, and their flowers are quite unbeatable. The single-flowered camellia species are my favorites, but the doubles have great charm, as do those like *C. japonica* 'Contessa Lavinia Maggi,' with striped pink and white many-petaled flowers. I have used camellias in impossibly dark courtyards and wells, and been astonished at their resilience.

ABOVE *A tiny, paved garden filled with interesting plants: blue and white* Agapanthus *nod their globular heads, while* Eucomis *displays its shapely leaves and unusual flowers.* Rhodochiton atrosanguineus *is trained up a pole to add height.*

Planning a courtyard

Courtyards have the benefit of walls, though their drawback is that, being enclosed, they are often dark. However, there is a host of plants that flourish in dark situations, requiring only good-sized containers, water and food to thrive.

The glazed pots made in the Far East are some of the finest containers for dark areas, with their light-reflecting glaze, which is entirely frost-proof. The largest ones are particularly good for standards, their bowl shape accentuating the mophead above. Standard hollies, created from a sturdy bush with care and patience, or bought as a treat from an enterprising nursery, do well in shady, enclosed yards. To give height and joy to a sunny yard, you could choose the extravagant standard fuchsias, pouring out their frilly explosions of color with prodigal splendor.

You might decide to be adventurous with a dark courtyard. For example, you could have brick arches set against the blank facing wall, with outdoor mirrored glass fixed within. There could even be a wall fountain trickling into a basin, with ferns and hostas in pots at its feet. A pair of standard bay trees or hollies, placed either side of the fountain and reflected in the mirrored arch, would look quite simple and stunningly elegant.

A courtyard could be made into a retreat, needing little more than white-painted walls and gravel underfoot, with planting spaces left for bamboo, such as *Arundinaria murielae* and *A. variegata*, the

PLANTS FOR DARK COURTYARDS

Acer palmatum

Aucuba

Camellia

Euonymus 'Silver Queen'

X *Fatshedera lizei*

Fatsia japonica

Ferns (many species)

Hedera (many species)

Hosta (many species)

Hydrangea (many species)

Impatiens

Skimmia japonica

Skimmia rubella

Viburnum tinus

dug-out holes being recovered with gravel after planting. A raised-container water garden could be placed in the center, with a wide enough surround to form a seat, and with *Nymphaea* pygmy water lilies and water iris in special pots, and *Cyperus alternifolius* for the summer.

Not all courtyards and paved areas are dark, of course. A sunnier courtyard or terrace might have walls up which you could grow climbers and thus create a three-tiered garden (see following pages). On a sunny patio, used for sitting out in warm weather, containers filled with fragrant flowers and foliage are irresistible (see page 97).

Among the plants that tolerate the dark conditions often imposed by courtyards are *Fatsia japonica* and several *Aucuba japonica* cultivars: 'Croto-nifolia,' 'Fructu Albo,' 'Picturata,' 'Sulphurea,' 'Variegata' or, the oldest of all, 'Maculata.' The Japanese maple, *Acer palmatum*, comes in a bewildering variety of delicate leaves and interesting, gnarled winter twigs, including the cultivars 'Elegans,' 'Elegans Purpureum,' 'Senkaki,' and 'Dissectum Atropurpureum,' the latter with a rounded, deeply cut mound of deep purple leaves that brighten to scarlet in the autumn, even in a shady situation. Camellias will even continue flowering bravely and putting on new growth in an overshadowed internal courtyard, where overhead building cuts out all possibility of light.

FAR LEFT *In this minimalist treatment of a courtyard, the overall impression is of a cool, peaceful retreat. Pots are used to enliven this corner and the white tobacco plant (*Nicotiana*) flowers even under the shade of the tree.*

LEFT *This is a joyous example of how invaluable* Impatiens *are in a dark, sunless courtyard. The large old urn, filled with* Impatiens *in splendidly mixed colors, brings a vibrant touch to the shadowy arch. Provided they are well watered, they will flower brightly for several months, even in shade.*

A sunny courtyard

This protected, south-facing courtyard is reached through French doors. The climbing rose against the wall would flourish for some years, and could be removed when it starts flagging. The long-term shrubs—*Ceanothus* and *Pittosporum*—could have a clematis planted nearby to wander through them. The mixture of containers is attractive in an informal setting, and space is allowed for extra colorful bedding each season. Planting in the urns at the top of the steps would also be changed seasonally.

Planting ideas for paved areas

Summer plantings
Fuchsia 'Kwintet,'
trained as standard;
Petunia Eagle Series
(left).
Acer palmatum
'Dissectum
Atropurpureum';
Convolvulus cneorum;
Verbena 'Sissinghurst';
Pelargonium
'Appleblossom
Rosebud' (right).

Single containers can have as much impact as pairs or groups of pots when used successfully to break up an expanse of paving; their positioning is all-important. Whether you have an enclosed courtyard, a small patio or a spacious terrace, look critically at the space available before placing a single pot, and plan how to use it to best effect.

Planting for a terrace

If paving runs right up to the house walls, have the largest containers between the door and the windows; these could hold climbers or scented plants, but the standard fuchsias shown here would be effective. Another group of three pots, asymmetrically set, might be all you need on a small terrace.

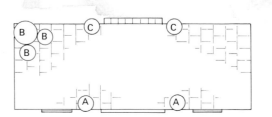

The standard fuchsias (A) are by the door, the group of three pots (B) in a corner, and one of these (C) marks the steps.

Winter plantings
Ilex aquifolium 'J.C.
Van Tol,' trained as a
half-standard;
Universal Plus pansies
(left).
Salix caprea; *Arbutus
unedo*; *Hedera helix*
'Anna Marie' (right).

Planting for a courtyard

If your whole garden is paved, and bounded
by walls, make your container groupings form
a visual barrier, preventing the total picture
from being seen all at once. If the containers
are well and thickly planted, they form a
screen through which the boundary can only
be glimpsed. Almost a winding path is

suggested, behind which there might be a
secret sitting-out area or a sunbathing spot.
The pots can be moved around according to
taste and social life, lined against the edge for
a party, and with less successful or "resting"
plantings hidden behind more showy ones.

It is important to plant for permanence in

both these schemes—a courtyard, like a
terrace, is visible all year round and should
always have some interest, such as that
provided by the variegated holly and the
strawberry tree (*Arbutus unedo*) in the
plantings shown here.

Using the walls

If your paved space is enclosed, the ideal solution is to build raised beds against all or just one of the perimeter walls. You could thus create a three-tiered effect of greenery to enhance your paved yard with climbers clothing the walls, shrubs and bedding forming mounds in the beds, and trailers tumbling over the raised front down to the ground.

If raised beds are kept low, say 15 in. high, they can be one-brick deep, topped with half-a-brick on edge; drainage holes should be made in the base and a good layer of crocks laid in the completed bed before you fill in with soil. A finished bed of 36 in. from front to back can easily support three major shrubs, as well as bulbs, bedding plants or perennial subjects.

Regular management of this type of container planting is important—all the climbers will try to grow forward and smother the middle layer which, in turn, tries to lie on the plants at the front and prevent them trailing down. Tie all climbers firmly to the wall or trellis behind, and watch constantly their tendency to outgrow and outflank. Remove whole branches of over-exuberant specimens, and the tops of others. You might, for example, have *Actinidia kolomikta* climbing up the wall, with its pink and green white-tipped leaves spreading out,

Berberis 'Rose Glow' in the middle and *Iberis sempervirens* falling down the front. In this instance, the *Actinidia* would need to be tied, bent sideways and pruned, to remain within the scope of your wall; the *Berberis* should be tied to a well-hidden stake, with the ties low enough to keep its main stem upright; and the *Iberis* will only need to have its bottom level clipped when it reaches the ground.

For maximum effect in a courtyard that is visible all year round, try to have a background of evergreen climber with perhaps a patio rose in the middle and silver foliage to trail. Alternatively, choose a deciduous climber, a strong foliage plant in the center— say, a *Phormium tenax*, a *Daphne odora* 'Aureomarginata' or a *Helleborus corsicus*—with campanula, helianthemum or *Viola cornuta* for the front runner. Any roses chosen for a small courtyard should always be the pillar type rather than true climbers, unless the walls are very high. The long new shoots of climbing roses, either stiff or too bendy, are difficult to control in small areas, whereas an amenable pillar rose is perfect; my favorite is 'Aloha,' profusely covered in its delectable scented, old-fashioned, pink-shading-to-coral flowers.

Climbers for enclosed gardens

For a sheltered, south- or west-facing position, nothing compares with *Solanum jasminoides* 'Album,'

BELOW, LEFT *This integrated raised bed, with a slatted-wood front to match the wooden decking, allows plenty of space for plants. Jasmine and* Solanum jasminoides *are trained against the trellis and the bed also holds a* Fatsia japonica, Erysimum *'Bowles' Mauve,'* Argyranthemum *'Jamaica Primrose,'* Teucrium fruticans, Cotoneaster horizontalis *'Variegata' and* Helichrysum italicum.

BELOW *In this enclosed garden, the plants soften the brick pillars and create an exciting composition of spikes, using* Cordyline, Phormium, Yucca *and* Aucuba japonica.

A raised bed makes the most of planting in a small, enclosed space. This large bed built in stone provides ample space for roses and foxgloves (Digitalis) among others, with bright pots of Argyranthemum, including the yellow 'Jamaica Primrose' placed in front.

placed side by side; in a container, they would flourish only if the container was substantial.

Another semi-tender, sweet-scented evergreen climber suitable for sheltered, sunny courtyards is *Trachelospermum jasminoides*. It flowers in mid-summer, smells delectable and has a neat, cheerful appearance that is entirely pleasing against a sunny wall. It can be placed in a pot on a porch, or beneath a canopy or sitting area to give it some protection. I have it in a sheltered raised bed with a rosemary protecting its feet.

Jasmines make good courtyard plants. *Jasminum officinale* 'Grandiflorum' requires a good-sized wall but does not resent ruthless pruning; *Jasminum nudiflorum* enjoys a north wall, adaptable to tumbling as well as climbing, with cheering yellow flowers in winter. *Jasminum revolutum* is superb for a large courtyard, its evergreen presence a useful, bulky filler against a wall, with yellow flowers over a long period in early summer. It requires watching for its smothering tendencies and can become too solid, but does not object to the pruning knife. *Jasminum primulinum*, with smaller evergreen leaves and yellow summer flowers, is less invasive; it does well in quite sheltered places.

Vines, particularly *Vitis vinifera* 'Purpurea,' make good pot-grown climbers and *V. vinifera* 'Brandt' produces sweet grapes which can be rescued from birds if you are quick and ingenious. *Vitis coignetiae*, the non-fruiting vine whose vast leaves and tendril-tipped arms constantly threaten me as I write, turns a magnificent scarlet in autumn, making a dramatic contribution to the effects of this season.

The deciduous climber, *Actinidia chinensis*, sends up enormous arms covered in huge, hairy leaves; though it may not sound very alluring, it looks spectacular climbing up the walls of a house. The hairy, almost prickly olive-silver leaves of *Fremontodendron californicum* remain on it all year and it is covered in extraordinarily cheering bright yellow flowers all summer. It is ideal for a large and sheltered area, or where it can be viewed from a distance, providing a brilliant cheering flash. It is very fast-growing and its root system is shallow, so it requires a substantial stake and strong wall ties to keep it securely in position.

a tender evergreen with glossy leaves, producing its delicate white flowers with yellow anthers from late spring through to the first frosts. In an open position it might not survive a bad winter, but in a town garden protected by the warmth of buildings, it flourishes. I have it rambling through a large *Pittosporum tobira*, waving about over the top and a constant joy all summer. Its fellow, *Solanum crispum* 'Glasnevin,' is also excellent, its blue-mauve potato flowers borne freely for most of the summer. It requires more pruning than *S. jasminoides* 'Album,' being more vigorous and inclined to smother its neighbors if not watched. It also provides a partner for a clematis, such as *Clematis* 'Alba Luxurians,' *C. viticella* 'Purpurea Plena Elegans,' *C. florida* 'Sieboldii,' or the spring-flowering *C. macropetala* or *C. alpina* cultivars. In a raised bed, these could be

LEFT *Pots of pink* Impatiens *and pelargoniums grow well in this sunny position by the cottage door. They flower prolifically and can be popped in front of plants past their best to keep a display going.*

RIGHT *Precision-clipped box hedges enclose neatly grouped pots holding topiarized box and a standard lilac, in the shade of magnificent* Catalpa *trees. These plants are all the more stylish for being perfectly groomed and maintained by regular clipping.*

Shade-loving ferns and hostas nestle in their pots against the wall by the front door to welcome visitors.

Front gardens

A paved front garden offers a tremendous challenge, all too often ignored. Consider that you pass through it several times a day and that it may be the only part of your garden that other people ever see. Not only could it give pleasure to friends, but inspiration and enjoyment to passersby.

In a large garden, where you have a drive or turning place for cars, thought has obviously to be given to the vehicles and their cargo, but there is no need to leave the front door unadorned. Consider placing a pair of handsome urns either side, with spectacular planting. Keep them pristine all year round, choosing a formal design using either superb camellias, standard bay trees, standard roses, well-cut hollies or well-grown *Acer* for a shady entrance. If the aspect is sunny, fill the urns with the best mixed planting at all times.

Strong planting for a small space

A small town front garden is often no more than a strip bordered with a fence or railing, and a few steps between street and door. This is no excuse to neglect it: towns need every scrap of greenery they can get to combat pollution. If your space is covered in bumpy concrete, lay gravel all over it to add interest and combat the unevenness and invest in one good, heavy urn on a pedestal. Plant it with a *Cordyline australis*, surrounded by *Felicia amelloides*, petunias or trailing pelargoniums. Alternative schemes that you might try could include a *Choisya ternata* and *Vinca major* 'Elegantissima'; *Convolvulus cneorum*; *Abelia grandiflora*; a box ball or other topiary shape; a small conifer surrounded by *Heuchera* 'Greenfinch'; a mass of ferns; a hydrangea; a pittosporum.

It is important in this situation to stick to simplicity—one good-sized shrub rather than several small ones; bedding in one or at the most two colors;

architectural plants rather than softer shapes. Whatever you choose, make sure the urn is well watered
and pampered; if you use bedding plants, whisk
them away directly when they are past their best; if a
shrub outgrows its pot, repot it in a larger container
or get another shrub.

Chimney pots are another container well adapted
to front gardens—their height places them at elbow
level or higher, and you can cheat by finding a
flowerpot which fits exactly into the top, making
seasonal planting easy. Chimney pots with castellated tops make a pleasant pun, and they enhance
trailers and spiky plants well.

Front gardens fall into the category of deserving
treats, and if your front garden is contained, while
the true garden lies behind, you can indulge in even
more extravagant combinations of tulips, lilies,
special narcissi or specimen shrubs. For a completely
different approach, a neat line of good, plain terra-

cotta pots with trained box balls, ending with one
box corkscrew, would be both stylish and effectively
simple.

One of the most effective front gardens I know has
a hedge of *Buxus sempervirens* 'Elegantissima' cut low
and square, with half-standards of *Euonymus fortunei
radicans* 'Silver Edge' rising from it, planted in gaps
in the paving. A yew hedge runs the other side of the
path, and a raised bed surrounding the paved center
is filled with *Choisya ternata*. The raised bed along
the front boundary has standard bay trees clipped to
lollipops and a hedge of *Skimmia japonica* at their
feet. An elegant stone urn on a pedestal sits in the
middle of the paving, filled with white bedding
plants and dangling silver ivy. Maintenance is
minimal, apart from watering, and the mixture of
greens, silver and white is enhanced by the weath-
ered stone paving and the white stucco of this formal
town house.

*A tall chimney pot
filled with bright
tulips would
cheer up any front
garden in spring.*

Window boxes

Ophiopogon planiscapus 'Nigrescens'

At first glance this plant may seem a small clump of black grass, but further study reveals the shining, polished detail on the flat leaves, the different angles at which they fall, and the way light strikes some and turns them deep purple. Soft pink flowers are borne on upright stems, knobbly and sculpted, in summer.

Unlike most container schemes, window boxes are designed to be seen from the street. This makes the choice of material more critical, since the box should complement the façade of the house or apartment, and the planting also has to be tackled in a rather different way. But before even buying a window box, let alone plants for it, inspect the position you plan to put it in and think about safety. If your windowsill has an elegant cast-iron guard in front of it, you can go ahead happily. If the sill is wide, and lower than the bottom of your window, allowing plenty of room to set a box or trough away from the wood, and still leaving space in front, once more you are safe.

In common with many gardeners, I have to confess to being thoroughly opinionated, both in relation to the choice of these containers and, to a degree, their occupants. Window boxes made of wood, terra-cotta or top-quality fiberglass are, to my mind, infinitely preferable to the plastic varieties found so easily in garden centers. Made in unhealthy shades of green, dark brown or dirty white, these containers never age, only crumble and become more unsightly as they grow older. However, fitted into a wood sleeve, they become both practical and good-looking; being lightweight, they can be filled and transported to a windowsill more easily than a heavy terra-cotta box, which would have to be filled *in situ*.

Another important consideration with window boxes is the maintenance they require. If you quail at the thought of trotting to and fro with a watering can, opening the windows and watering the boxes every day in the summer, and finding someone to take over when you go on vacation, do not have window boxes. Nothing in container gardening looks sadder than troughs of spiky, dead objects stuck outside the windows of an otherwise handsome house. Unless they are watered, fed and occasionally cut back and dead-headed, plants in window boxes simply do not flourish, and the trouble is that they really are on display.

When several window boxes are placed in the same façade, uniformity is needed to produce the best result. Six boxes, all different, up and down the same frontage would distract the eye rather than please it. Even when planted with identical and matching plants, they will grow slightly differently and display enough variation to satisfy. Provided the boxes themselves are identical, they can be planted with different groupings of the same colors, or different numbers of the same plants, but there must be uniformity of selection, especially in a formal setting. Do not ignore the possibilities of an all-

Fixing a window box

If you have only a rudimentary sill, with bare wall below your window, consider installing strong metal brackets below window level, which will allow you to plant solidly without losing light in the room. When setting a trough on a windowsill, raise it on low half-bricks or pieces of slate, high enough to allow air to get through and water to drain away. It may be sufficient to jam wooden wedges underneath to keep it upright, but check regularly that they are not rotting away. Never stand an untethered pot on a sill.

Fix the brackets to the wall properly, bearing in mind the weight of a wet, filled box (below).

Fix wire under the rim of a plastic box and attach the ends to hooks in the window frame.

green theme, or green with variegated foliage: set against a white or cream wall, it can look distinguished. Its impact would, indeed, be lessened by including colored flowers.

Planting a window box

Window boxes, more than other containers, lend themselves to purely seasonal planting and for this reason require more rigorous renewing than do more permanent displays. Since windowsills are relatively shallow, few window boxes are made deeper than 12 in. from back to front. It therefore becomes necessary to renew the soil frequently; and to replace the plants entirely each season. Guidelines for planting a box are given on page 25.

Scale is a vital consideration in window box planting. When a box is seen against a large wall, ensure that there is height in the selection, either in the center (provided, perhaps, by a *Cordyline australis*), or at the sides, in the form of dwarf conifers. Bear in mind, however, that too much height in the middle, or too successful growth throughout the whole box can darken the room within. As you plan out your planting scheme, remember that it is designed primarily to be seen from the outside. You will not be able to make it as interesting visually from within, but, if you can, try to ensure that the color scheme blends with that of the interior or at least does not jar with it. If you include some scented species (see page 97), you will be able to enjoy the benefit of their perfume wafting into the room when the window is open.

ABOVE *This well-planted window box displays a splendid mass of small flowers set against contrasting foliage. The purple leaves of* Begonia semperflorens *combine with the variegated* pelargonium *and* Glechoma *leaves and daisy flowers of* Brachyscome *with taller* Arctotis *to give height to the scheme.*

Winter and summer window boxes

Limited only by size and aspect, window box planting can create a marvelous antidote to city gloom. One of the great charms of this form of container gardening is the chance to experiment—to play with colors, textures and shapes; to be restrained and somber or wildly colorful and extravagant. My own preference is generally for a limited color range, with foliage playing a vital part. Here we consider schemes for winter and for summer, with contrasting aspects. The same window box, measuring 36 in. × 9 in. and 8 in. deep is used for each scheme, painted to match the house front. (A planting plan for a spring trough is given on page 88.)

Winter sun
Buxus sempervirens, clipped to balls; *Eucalyptus gunnii*; *Hedera helix* 'Golden Jubilee' (left).

Winter shade
Cupressus elwoodii; *Euonymus fortunei* 'Silver Queen'; *Aucuba japonica* 'Maculata'; *Hedera helix* 'Green Ripple'; Universal Plus pansies (below).

Winter scheme for a sunny sill

This scheme would look good in a formal setting. The *Eucalyptus gunnii*, started as young plants, should be kept cut back to retain their juvenile foliage. The box balls should be clipped annually. It would be essential to replenish the topsoil and to feed generously if these plants are left *in situ* for over a year.

Winter scheme for shade

The miniature cypresses give height to the scheme and could remain in the box, while the aucubas, put in as young plants, could stay for only one winter, or at the most two. The white-margined foliage of the euonymus is echoed by the white pansies.

Summer shade
Fatsia japonica;
Saxifraga × urbium;
Hedera helix 'Eva' (left).

Summer sun
Lonicera nitida
'Baggesen's Gold';
Salvia farinacea
'Victoria'; *Verbena*
Derby Series; *Viola*
'*Ardross Gem*';
Helichrysum petiolare
'Limelight'; *Lobelia
erinus* 'Light Blue
Basket' (below).

Summer scheme for shade

If the *Fatsia japonica* is put in as a young plant, it could remain for several years. The thick cluster of London pride (*Saxifraga × urbium*), with its rosettes of flowers in summer, positively needs protection from sunlight. (*Impatiens* would also flower profusely even in shade.) Variegated ivy softens the edge of the box.

Summer scheme for the sun

The two *Lonicera nitida* should be well-grown plants, taken from cuttings, and clipped to form tall pyramids. They could remain in the box, with bedding and soil changed seasonally around them. If the violas are cut right back in mid-summer, they should continue flowering into autumn.

Hanging baskets

At their best, hanging baskets can be magnificent, their extravagant mass of color and foliage adding a sumptuous new dimension to walls and doorways. Equally, they can be mingy, ugly and unsuitable: dirty plastic shapes filled with dying lobelias and dead ivies hung in inappropriate places, where they are tone-lowering and unlovely.

The secret of splendor lies, yet again, in scale, coupled with suitability. The very artificiality of hanging baskets places them ideally in a particular setting—against cottage walls, on balconies, roof gardens, in porches, around swimming pools or conservatories—and makes them entirely unsuitable for others, such as against a period doorway or in a formal grand design. Some of the most impressive hanging baskets are in fact seen in an urban or semi-urban context, hanging bright and sparkling from lampposts, or pouring voluptuously down the front of a restaurant or wine bar.

The billowing splendor of this hanging basket shows how fully they should be planted. The plants—in this case petunias, trailing lobelia, pelargoniums and Helichrysum petiolare—hide the basket completely.

Hanging baskets have some rigid requirements and criteria; if these are attended to, they become a joy and delight. First, you should choose the largest basket you can fit into the available space. Choose a completely plain hanging basket, without curly plastic bits, unless you are moving into the domain of Victorian wirework and their effective modern copies. The former are suitable for all the positions mentioned, the latter can be an additional treat for conservatory or terrace.

Next comes the sphagnum moss or its alternatives for the conservation-minded: always buy more than you expect to use, because a successful hanging basket should have all its components hidden by plant material. For the planting medium, choose the ready-made mixture of a peat moss- or peat moss-substitute-based compost with additional water-retentive granules. Instructions for planting a hanging basket are given on page 26.

SUCCESSFUL PLANT COMBINATIONS

Fuchsias, lobelias and petunias in harmonious shades;

Helichrysum petiolare 'Limelight' with *Felicia amelloides* 'Variegata';

Tolmeia menziesii alone;

Primula malacoides on top, with small-leaved ivies all around;

Dorotheanthus (mesembryanthemums);

Begonias in all forms and colors, good for shade;

Tradescantia pendula;

Osteospermum 'Whirligig' with *Felicia amelloides*;

Argyranthemum 'Jamaica Primrose,' with pale blue trailing lobelia and parsley.

Plants for hanging baskets

The choice of plants and color is, of course, very personal. Some will prefer a riot of clashing, startling colors: scarlet pelargoniums, orange marigolds, purple hanging verbena, blue trailing lobelia; others will fill a basket with *Helichrysum petiolare* and nothing else, making a frilly, silvery shape to set against a dark background. A single choice of plant can in fact be tremendously effective: imagine one huge mass of *Convolvulus mauritanicus*, pouring its violet-blue trumpets down against a white wall; or a tumbling heap of brilliant nasturtiums; a spreading tangle of trailing verbena; a globe of *Impatiens*; a delicate tracery of ferns for shade.

In general for hanging basket schemes, plants whose natural habit is to trail and tumble are most likely to appeal. These include: ivy-leaved pelargoniums, fuchsias, lobelias, verbenas, campanulas, begonias, sedums, alyssum, aubrietas, alpine phlox, saxifrages, felicias, *Convolvulus cneorum*, *C. tricolor*, *C. minor*, candytuft, coleus, pansies and violas and, of course, the foliage plants: small ivies and ferns, *Lysimachia* and many silver-leaved plants, including *Helichrysum petiolare* 'Cassinia Ward's Silver.' Color selections and blending are vital considerations here and some of the most tasteful combinations include those listed on the opposite page.

After-care

Consider carefully the location of your hanging basket, bearing in mind that few passersby will appreciate a dowsing from above. Make sure it will remain where you intend it to—remember the combined weight of wet soil, plants and the container, and the way the wind roars around city corners seeking the unfastened and lightly fettered. Check that the hooks supporting your hanging basket are properly secured into the wall and the chains firmly attached to the basket's rim.

Once your basket is hung in position, it will need a thorough watering just about every single day, or at least on alternate days. There are now excellent devices to deal with this. Either suspend your basket

on pulley hangers, which can be raised or lowered as needed, enabling you to put your watering can or slow-running hose right onto the basket's surface. Otherwise invest in the special long-arm attachment designed for high-level watering which is a life-saver if you have several hangers and some window boxes. Each week, in summer, add a weak liquid fertilizer to your watering arrangements, tapering off at the end of summer.

More than any other container, a hanging basket requires grooming; its blowsy tendency is part of its charm, but it must be controlled enough to create a huge, billowing globe of color or foliage, unsullied by dying bits or dead flowers. Check, as the season progresses, that soil has not leached away, and top it up if needed; use scissors regularly to dead-head, to remove surplus foliage, and to trim.

The combination of a very limited color range, which enhances the old stone walls, with well-shaped foliage of Tolmiea menziesii *to balance the glorious flowers of petunias, begonias and white lobelia, produces an excellent hanging basket.*

SUCCESSFUL PLANTING

Suiting the plants to their container, both to its form and the material of which it is made, is as important as matching the containers to their locations. In this chapter we take a close look at successful schemes for containers. The second part of the chapter takes a tantalizing glimpse at specialist aspects of growing plants in containers. This covers not only the more obvious examples of special needs, such as growing acid-loving subjects like azaleas or camellias in special acidic compost, but also the role of tubs and pots in growing alpines, producing a kitchen garden on a small scale, or being turned into a water garden.

This exuberant collection of sun-loving flowers and foliage makes an exciting corner in a warm, sheltered garden. Spiky Agave americana 'Marginata' defines the froth of flowers all around, backed by the deep purple rosettes of Aeonium arboreum 'Zwartkop.' Colors are limited, the shapes varied and the style informal.

The best use of containers

The successful use of containers depends, as we have seen, partly on their suitability for the location and partly on the choice of complementary and well-balanced plant material. But the number and position of containers is also of great importance and grouping them together in a pleasing and harmonious way requires special care. As a general guide, pairs and single large-scale plantings indicate formality, whereas clusters and gatherings of pots do the opposite, conveying an informal air.

A single container, well planted with a good balance of plant material, can stand alone if it is large and important enough; can be paired for a formal statement; or can become part of a group. Three or four pots standing in a row, evenly spaced on a large terrace, with each one making its own statement, will be successful in a formal way.

Certain large containers can have great impact left unplanted, provided they are correctly placed. In this context they become ornaments in themselves, such as the giant Ali Baba jar, set on paving as the centerpiece for an herb garden, or the antique urn on a pedestal, a triumphant focal point that is too beautiful to require more than sky to set it off. The superbly thrown pot, perhaps in a salt glaze, needs no more than planting at its feet to enhance its coloring. A black ceramic pot could have a carpet of delicious *Ophiopogon planiscapus* 'Nigrescens' at its base in summer.

A pair of matching containers gives style and impact, as well as conferring a degree of formality. If you want to draw attention to an arch, a pergola, a gateway or a flight of steps, a pair at either side will do the job more effectively than one alone (see pages 40–43). Conversely, if you have a change of level in a country-cottage garden, massed pots of different sizes and shapes, filled informally, will set the right mood as well as draw attention.

This pair of matching standard daisy bushes (Argyranthemum frutescens) are sophisticated in their simplicity. They can be bought like this or trained into a standard at home. Confining their roots and generous feeding will encourage prolific flowering.

The right scale

Scale is of the utmost importance when it comes to putting a group of containers together, because no impact can be worth its salt unless it is carefully considered and balanced. A well-filled group of three terra-cotta pots of varying height and shape, for example, will make a statement that is well worth attention; two small, messily planted ones will never have the same effect.

The question of scale is equally critical when it comes to planting up your containers. Minginess is death to good planting, whether of pot or plant, so always aim for larger rather than smaller, bearing in mind the space you have available, and avoid mean plantings—lonely, unfed little souls skulking in a skimpy pot. Gardeners always have a tendency to be generous, both to their plants and to each other: join this cheerful band and learn to think expansively when you are planning your containers.

ABOVE *A trough of* Diascia *and pots of daisies, lilies and* Verbena *'Sissinghurst' in the small urn form an ebullient, colorful and well-chosen group for an informal setting.*

RIGHT *The simple lines of this perfectly positioned single stone pot draw the eye to the soft white flowers of the lacecap hydrangea.*

Successful schemes

The container plantings which give us the greatest pleasure all have one thing in common and that is harmony, in one form or another. Either the plants themselves are completely harmonious, or they and their container form a complementary whole. Balance is one important component of a successful planting, color and shape another, scale a third.

Selecting plant material requires discrimination and ruthlessness, and combining it successfully with your container calls for a sense of style. Developing an eye for style comes from experience—the more different types of pot and tub you have used in the past, the easier it becomes to choose and integrate your container plants. It is a good idea to look at a few distinctly different shapes of container and consider complementary plant material, for which suggestions are given on the following pages. But the advice I give on design aspects can only be a starting point for your own voyage of discovery.

ABOVE *The shapely ribbed leaves of hostas make them an ideal complement for plain, round pots. Here, a golden variegated and a white-margined hosta are spiked by orange-flowered Calceolaria (Bikini Series).*

FAR LEFT *The height of this standard variegated holly is balanced by the bright winter pansies.*

LEFT *Sedums make a satisfying shape and are best appreciated, as here, in a low, shallow pan.*

This excellent combination shows a master plantswoman at work. Height, variety, exuberance and taste all feature in this generously planted container: Abutilon 'Canary Bird,' Bidens aurea and the vivid Helichrysum petiolare 'Limelight' make a balanced composition which has great impact.

Melianthus major
This marvelously architectural South African plant arrived in Europe in the seventeenth century. Its jagged-edged leaves arch out gracefully. A mature specimen contains every shade in the glaucous spectrum, changing and shimmering as light strikes each curve of the leaves. In a sunny corner it will sprawl luxuriantly—aromatic and impossibly beautiful.

Matching plant shapes to containers

When starting to plant a pot, or a group of containers from scratch, either your container comes first, or a particular plant, seldom both at once. Whatever your starting point, the plants must complement the pot, or vice versa. Here we look at the basic shape of various familiar types of container and consider complementary plants for them. (The traditional "flowerpot" in terra-cotta, stone or composition is not covered here since it is an easy shape that can be planted successfully with almost any mixture of plants, including trees and shrubs.)

Wide-mouthed, deep bowl

This shape is a versatile one, able to set off a formal or informal tree, shrub or annual with equal success. These pots are very often glazed ceramic, and come in attractive colors such as deep blue, pale turquoise, blue-gray and warm brown. The decorated ones blend with bamboos, palms, *Acer palmatum*, *Brugmansia*, *Hoya* and grasses.

Caisse Versailles

This classic square box demands a standard, half-standard, topiary or clipped tree or shrub. The central tree or shrub may be underplanted or not. While these containers can be extremely versatile, height must always be a component.

Suitable plants for training as standards include *Laurus nobilis* (bay), *Buxus sempervirens*

(box), *Prunus lusitanica* (Portuguese laurel), *Ligustrum* (privet), some *Cupressus*, *Elaeagnus*, *Fuchsia*, *Heliotropium*, *Argyranthemum frutescens*, and *Lantana camara*.

While it is relatively easy to create a standard tree or shrub yourself, provided you have time and patience (see pages 34–35), the corkscrew shape needs to be carefully trained around a stake. But these and other specimens can be bought as a treat.

Classical vase

This shape demands an upright centerpiece, something trailing over the sides, and a clump or group to fill the middle. The plants used in such a composition should have an

affinity in color—either all bold or all soft —or a conscious juxtaposition of the two as contrasts.

Suitable upright evergreen foliage plants include *Cordyline*, *Phormium* or *Yucca*, while flowering plants with an upright habit may be chosen from *Fuchsia*, *Heliotropium*, some *Salvia*, *Cineraria*, *Agapanthus*, *Tulip* or a *Lantana camara*.

For the clump-forming middle group of plants, choose from *Pelargonium*, *Argyranthemum*, *Fuchsia*, some *Salvia*, *Eschscholzia*, some *Begonia*, dwarf *Tulip*, *Polyanthus*, *Auricula*, *Zinnia*, *Aster*, *Dianthus*, *Myosotis* and daisies such as *Bellis perennis*.

Suitable trailing plants include *Helichrysum petiolare*, *Petunia*, the trailing forms of *Pelargonium*, *Fuchsia* and *Lobelia*, *Campanula*, *Hedera*, some *Sedum*, some *Artemisia*, *Lysimachia nummularia*, *Amaranthus candatus*, *Diascia*, *Viola*, *Felicia*, some *Begonia*, *Osteospermum*, *Tradescantia*, some *Verbena*, *Heliotropium*, *Helianthemum*, *Origanum*, *Aubrieta*, *Sempervivum*, *Alyssum*, *Saponaria*, *Tanacetum*, and *Salvia chamaedryoïdes*.

Giant oil jars

These containers, often known as Ali Baba jars, are wonderfully alluring both empty and planted. They can equally well be planted with trailers or something with a bold outline for contrasts.

Trailers include the smaller cultivars of clematis such as *Clematis macropetala* (shown here), or *C. alpina*, ivies with medium-sized leaves such as *Hedera helix* 'Sagittifolia,' *Helichrysum petiolare* 'Limelight,' *Vinca*, *Tropaeolum peregrinum*, *Lysimachia nummularia*, *Humulus lupulus* 'Aureus,' *Solanum jasminoides* 'Album,' *Trachelospermum jasminoides*, *Ipomoea*, *Hoya*, *Rhodochiton atrosanguineum*, *Passiflora caeruleum*, *Cobaea scandens* or *columneas*.

For planting with a bold outline, consider bamboos, larger grasses, larger ferns, *Cordyline*, *Phormium*, *Yucca*, *Rhus typhina*, *Trachycarpus fortunei* or *Fatsia japonica*.

Wide, shallow bowl

Apart from their use for alpines, low bowls or troughs can be excellent for dotting bulbs or small bright plants such as *Viola*, *Sempervivum* and *Mesembryanthemum*, wherever color is needed at ground level.

Grouping containers

Grouping containers together in such a way that they have some impact requires a careful eye. The triangle, as we shall see, is the basis of many successful groupings since it offers great versatility. On a small terrace, viewed through a window, three pots grouped together in a rough triangle will produce an instant garden—provided, of course, that the plantings in each pot are harmonious in color, texture or both. Several examples of triangular groupings are given on these pages, all working in a completely different way. Where there is space for more than one grouping, the other important element to take into consideration, when you are grouping your containers, is the way in which groups of pots are juxtaposed and work within the outdoor space.

All groups are usually improved by having some contrast in height. You can achieve this quite simply either by using a tall shrub, small tree or standard in one of the containers, or by including in the group one pot that is taller than the others, such as an urn or chimney pot. All groups benefit from some flowing planting—for example, petunias and daisies mixed with trailing lobelias; lilies near cascading silver foliage; mixtures of upright and trailing pelargoniums; or massed and tumbling diascias, verbenas and gazanias.

RIGHT *In this early autumn group of terra-cotta pots, the standard* Argyranthemum frutescens *at the back balances the spiky* Cordyline *while the variegated* Hebe × andersonii *'Variegata' adds form at a lower level. Trailing ivies soften the overall composition, while cheerful pansies bring a touch of color.*

Triangular groups

The triangle grouping can take many forms, depending on your choice of containers. One pot—or one planting—standing higher than the rest will form the apex of the triangle, but this need not necessarily be the central component. Height can be achieved by using a tall container, an urn standing on a pedestal or by including a standard tree or shrub, or an upright species such as a *Cordyline* or *Phormium*.

If your dominant pot contains, for example, an enormous Japanese Fatsia (*Fatsia japonica*), with its bold, architectural leaves, you may set two low bowls of *Euonymus fortunei* 'Silver Queen' at either side, underplanting the *Fatsia* with variegated small-leaved ivy to echo and emphasize the subtlety of this foliage-only theme.

If you have a tall chimney pot shaped like a castle in chess, give it an enormous *Cordyline australis*, with clouds of pale blue lobelia pouring through the castellated top, and place it above an urn filled with white, large-flowered begonias, and beside a plain, gray-blue stoneware pot crammed with the bright golden grass *Hakonechloa macra* 'Aureola.'

Some plants always look better alone and will create more impact if used in that way. Hostas, with their rounded, fleshy-looking leaves, will lushly fill an ample pot and add style to any group. They blend superbly with the delicate fronds of ferns in an adjacent container—and both enjoy shady conditions. A standard daisy bush (*Argyranthemum frutescens*) in a classical Versailles box also looks effective when placed alone, or it can equally become the center of a cluster of well-filled pots planted with pelargoniums, daisies and small-leaved trailers, such as ivy, creeping Jenny, periwinkle (*Vinca*) or nepeta.

LEFT *The standard* Laurus nobilis *(sweet bay) on a twisted stem will have great impact throughout the year. This effect is created by training the stem of a young plant around a cane. With the bright azalea, backed by clipped box, a simple but stylish grouping is created.*

Year-round groupings

Grouping of containers offers plenty of scope, both to ring in changes and provide pleasant surprises. All plants have their best season, and those whose strength lies in their foliage extend the time considerably. When planning for different seasons of the year, make sure a group has enough permanent foliage to stand on its own without requiring flowers. An evergreen clump can look somber without color; introduce variegated foliage, or some silver to lighten the group even in winter. Add a deciduous shrub whose young foliage is a brilliant shrimp-pink or the brightest shade of green, like the Japanese maples; use the blue-gray of glaucous leaves (such as that of *Eucalyptus*) to throw both groups into relief.

Remember the bright leaf-tips of *Photinia* and *Pieris*; the pretty marbled pink of *Berberis thunbergii* 'Rose Glow' and *Fuchsia magellanica* 'Versicolor'; the glowing yellow of *Sambucus nigra* 'Aurea,' the lovely silver frills of *Artemesia*.

With the choice of plant species before you, it is easy to move your pots about, according to the season. Add the dimensions of height and shape before you think about flowers and scent. Some of the most effective groupings are different combinations of the same color spectrum; all foliage with, for example, yellow or golden tendencies, but in different forms, and spiked with the darkest greens. Study, too, the seasonal changes within groups of plants: the deepening of brilliantly striped hosta leaves; the autumn offering of flame and crimson.

RIGHT *This large group of assorted containers has strong contrasts of shape, texture and foliage color, with flowers merely a bonus. The rounded* Sedum *contrasts with the spikes of the* Agave *and* Cordyline australis, *and is softened by the daisy flowers of* Argyranthemum frutescens, *the* Pelargonium *and* Impatiens *and the felted foliage of* Helichrysum petiolare.

Group planting schemes

Ideas are given on these pages for a free-standing triangular group of three pots in varying sizes, which could equally well live on a patio, a roof garden or a terrace. Long-term planting is combined with spring bulbs and summer bedding for added interest in each season. One group is suitable for a sunny position, the other for shade. Plants have been chosen to enhance their pots and each one contributes to the group scheme in an individual way, while the overall effect is that of a harmonious whole.

Sunny Group
Aralia elata *'Variegata';*
Cupressus glabra
(trained as a standard)
with Petunia;
Phormium tenax
'Purpurea' with
Pelargonium
'L'Elégante,' Viola
'Belmont Blue,'
Verbena × hybrida
'Amethyst.'

Group of pots in the shade

In a shady position it is best to concentrate on plants which have interesting and attractive foliage with spots of colors dotted about.

Hostas create stylishly shaped pots of foliage wherever they are placed and the variegated *Hosta fortunei aureomarginata* dominates the group in the largest pot. Its heart-shaped leaves form a good contrast to the feathery foliage of ferns.

Shady Group
Hosta fortunei
aureomarginata;
Polystichum setiferum;
Begonia semperflorens.

Group for a sunny position

The *Aralia elata* 'Variegata' in the large pot (left) has enormous, finely cut, silvery variegated leaves; it is deciduous, becoming a knotted walking stick in winter. This plant is particularly good when viewed from above, as the older plants reach ever upward, forming a wonderfully elegant umbrella, and their charms are wasted on those at ground level.

This slow-growing tree is not suitable for pruning; it is very expensive to buy but a "treat" for the deserving.

The standard *Cupressus glabra* in the lower, wide container gives some solid, evergreen height to the group. It is underplanted with scilla bulbs, and spring bedding of auriculas is added, with bedding of white petunias in summer.

The wide-mouthed, tapering pot

completing the group contains a *Phormium tenax* 'Purpurea' which gives a dramatic outline at a lower level. Summer bedding in pastel shades includes trailing *Pelargonium* 'L'Elégante,' with soft pink pelargoniums, pale blue violas and pink trailing verbenas. For winter bedding, *Skimmia japonica* 'Rubella' is added and removed to another group, or to a place in the garden border, in spring.

Seasonal planting schemes

Citrus mitis
Dotted with flowers and fruit at the same time, with a ravishing scent, this is a dwarf cousin of the citrus trees growing in Mediterranean countries. The courtyards of Roman villas were filled with orange trees and, later, medieval monks made preserves from the fruits.

Every season in container gardening has its particular appeal and each offers a challenge. Summer is of course the height of the flowering season and this is generally the time when most displays in pots, troughs and window boxes look their best. But the best plantings have some interest all year round and both winter and spring have highlights of their own. Since summer planting schemes are well represented throughout the pages of this book, we pay particular attention here to schemes for often neglected seasons.

Planting for winter interest

However small, any contained garden must have some form of evergreen: a cluster of empty pots in winter would be a sad admission of failure. If your garden leans toward the formal, this essential ingredient could be a pair, or a single pot, of standardized box, privet, *Prunus lusitanica* (Portuguese laurel), euonymus, or a conifer; any topiarized shape in box, including corkscrew, mound, pyramid

or clipped topiary animal; or an ivy pyramid, pole or tree. Holly in all forms, plain or variegated, can be grown as an upright tree or topiarized. *Laurus nobilis*, the sweet bay, is a little tender in its topiarized form, requiring city protection or a milder climate, but is hardier left as a tree. A decorative pot of *Buxus elegantissima*, the silvery variegated box, makes a cheerful compromise between formal and informal—quite a small plant, if well fed, will grow fast enough to join in without looking silly within three years if you feed both roots and foliage.

If you are aiming for a more informal structure, the choice of evergreens is even wider. Choose from the following: *Rhamnus alaternus* 'Argenteovariegata,' *Arbutus unedo*, aucuba, camellia, *Fatsia japonica*, bamboos, pittosporum, ligustrum, olearia, *Osmanthus heterophyllus* 'Aureomarginatus,' *Daphne odora* 'Aureomarginata,' pieris, sarcococca, *Skimmia japonica* 'Rubella,' pyracantha, eucalyptus, photinia, euonymus, elaeagnus, conifers, including *Chamaecyparis lawsoniana*, hebe, ceanothus, *Viburnum tinus* and *V. tinus* 'Variegata,' and *Rhododendron yakushimanum* and its hybrids.

Bear in mind that a large container can often hold two shrubs, one evergreen and one deciduous, at least for some time. I kept an *Arbutus unedo* and a *Salix caprea* in a terra-cotta pot 19 in. in diameter and 21 in. high for five or six years with great success and only removed them when I was changing the design of the garden.

Any evergreen can of course be surrounded with winter bedding plants for seasonal interest, such as winter-flowering pansies or heathers (*Erica carnea* 'December Red' and 'Springwood White') if the soil is suitable. Greenhouse-grown cyclamen (*C. persicum*), produced commercially and sold in late autumn, are hardy in sheltered areas, flowering for over two months or longer, and could enhance an evergreen planting. Small, variegated-leaf ivies will trail attractively down the sides of any large container, softening its otherwise severe winter appearance: choose from *Hedera helix* 'Atropurpurea,' 'Parsley Crested' and 'Little Diamond.'

ABOVE *A few containers planted with spring bulbs provide the first, long-awaited signs of life in a garden. In a raised bed* Helleborus argutifolius *sets the scene and vivid yellow* Narcissus *'Tête à Tête,' some polyanthus and Universal Plus pansies carry it through to summer.*
OPPOSITE *Winter deserves brightening up too. Winter-flowering heathers (*Erica carnea*) are combined with ivy in a stone "basket."*

Spring planting schemes

Bulbs of various kinds can be considered in conjunction with different container planting schemes; instructions for planting them are given on page 24. It is fun to browse through bulb catalogs, gazing at the improbably gleaming, healthy flowers, and planning mixtures to suit your taste and pocket. The only problem usually lies in a shortage of unfilled pots and space at the time when the bulbs arrive. They turn up, plump and filled with promise, in autumn, when your pots are still full of shrubs or the last of the summer bedding—but all container gardening is dogged with this sort of challenge. If you have a large garden and enough pots to keep some free for this purpose, you are in an enviable position and must take advantage of it.

Lilies, tulips and hyacinths, in particular, seem to have a natural affinity with pots, and look good wherever they are placed. Some of the smaller bulbs, such as scillas, grape hyacinths, crocus and all the miniature narcissi are splendid assets in small gardens, besides providing wonderful alpine vistas. Snowdrops survive in my raised beds and peer through the early gloom with glee.

I find the larger daffodils difficult to manage in the container garden—they tend to flop too soon after opening their trumpets, and their dying foliage lacks charm and is impossible to hide in such small spaces. The small narcissi that I consider most successful, because they flower again, even lasting for three or four years, are: *Narcissus cyclamnineus, N. triandrus, N.* 'February Gold,' 'February Silver,' 'Jack Snipe,' 'Jenny,' 'Tête à Tête,' 'April Tears' and 'Minnow.' Provided you arrange a foliage shrub around them, to hide the dying leaves, and remember to feed them after they have flowered, they provide magical early spring brightness.

Tulips make particularly good window box dwellers, especially the *kaufmanniana* hybrid "Water lily" tulips, whose mottled and stripy foliage is an extra asset. The range of early double tulips have a wide color spectrum, and are neat and even in growth, making them suited to pot culture. Certain peony-flowered tulips are imposing; 'Mount Tacoma,' growing to a height of 20 in., is a beautiful pure white and, though it is tall for most pots, it looks magnificent and stately massed in a large lead cistern. Of the early single family, my favorite is 'Apricot Beauty,' whose subtle coloring blends perfectly with old terra-cotta. This tulip deserves to be displayed in a good urn or vase-shaped terra-cotta pot, with a few trails of small dark green ivy dangling at the sides.

Lilies, the most magical of all bulbs, thrive on pot life, and their majestic beauty, delectable scent and sheer, ravishing loveliness render them the queen of containers everywhere. There is a vast range of lilies, but *Lilium regale* is the easiest, longest-lasting and most manageable species, requiring no more than a good start. It is well worth getting a catalog to study from one of the bulb specialists.

Winter and spring planting ideas

Before embarking on a container garden, remind yourself that there is more to life than summertime. Determine from the start that your pots will flourish in winter and autumn, and bring enchantment to spring as well as to summer. Rely on the wealth of spring bulbs to provide early cheer to any outdoor scene. Choosing the right evergreens for winter entails thinking in terms of variegated or golden foliage, to take the place of flower color and to lift a group that is predominantly plain green. Learn about genera such as the *Pieris*, offering bright foliage followed by flowers, while its overall shape is stylish. Berries and flowers are provided by the skimmias, some viburnums, many hollies, aucubas, gaultherias and many more. Do not neglect the reliable glossy-leaved evergreens such as *Choisya ternata* and camellias, with their lovely flowers, and the various privets (*Ligustrum*); plant evergreen ferns and pamper decorative ivies and your winter garden will lighten your spirits.

Spring trough

This planting plan for a large trough, 36 in. long × 16 in. wide, relies largely on spring bulbs. The miniature juniperus give height and permanence to the overall scheme, but the iberis and euphorbia could also stay in the trough permanently. The grape hyacinths and narcissi could remain too, and would flower again for two or three years at least, if fed.

Iberis sempervirens; *Juniperus communis* 'Compressa'; *Euphorbia myrsinites*; *Tulipa fosteriana* 'Purissima'; *Narcissus* 'Thalia'; *Muscari*; *Myosotis* 'Royal Blue.'

Winter group

This group of pots features permanent planting but has been planned particularly with winter interest in mind. The young leaves of the pieris are a brilliant bronze-red even in the winter months; this dense, evergreen shrub has been underplanted with *Narcissus triandrus* and white hyacinths to add spring highlights to the group. The skimmia has aromatic red-edged foliage and red flower buds throughout autumn and winter that open to panicles of creamy white scented flowers in spring. The golden box forms a bright focal point all year round, but in winter its clipped yellow bun-shape is especially welcome.

Pieris formosa forrestii 'Wakehurst'; *Hedera helix* 'Glacier'; *Skimmia japonica* 'Rubella'; *Buxus sempervirens* 'Aurea.'

Special growing needs

Bold and beautiful, the Cordyline australis and Arctotis both enjoy coastal conditions and provide a note of tropical splendor. If they could spend the winter under glass for protection, they could be whisked out onto a sunny terrace each summer.

We have considered the best way of getting maximum fun and impact from our containers, including an element of planning, and striving for harmony and balance. Another facet of this irresistible subject is the flexibility factor and this offers a further dimension for the prospective gardener.

Whether the plants themselves have special needs, or the owners have specialist interests, growing in containers can often provide the answer. Those who find regular gardening beyond them, owners of restricted sites longing for fresh vegetables, devotees

of fairy-sized alpines, rhododendron-lovers living on chalk, retired coastal dwellers being buffeted by salt winds, and children unable to grub happily in real earth—all such challenges can be met by an army of suitably selected containers.

Lime-hating plants

The most obvious category of plants for which containers are essential are those that require a special diet. The group of plants which actively dislike any lime in their compost includes many favorite subjects, such as rhododendrons, azaleas, camellias, pieris, some heathers, *Kalmia latifolia*, pernettyas, *Cryptomeria japonica* 'Elegans,' magnolias and gentians. If they are grown in large containers of specially mixed acidic compost, they will thrive.

Where relevant, I have mentioned these lime-haters in context throughout the book, but it is important to remember them when planning a scheme and to combine them in pots with other acid-loving plants. Bear in mind their dislike of mushroom compost (containing a high lime content) and their preference for rainwater against tap water in hard-water districts. They should also be given regular doses of fertilizer specially formulated for acid-loving subjects.

Coastal gardening

Gardening by the sea, despite the milder climate, offers ordeal by wind to even matters up a little. Salt-laden coastal winds can be ferocious and frequent, and plants in coastal gardens need a robust attitude to survive—and additional attributes to flourish. But with the correct choice of tolerant, hardy plants, the container garden by the sea can be as pleasurable as one in a more protected site.

Shelter, obviously, is a prime consideration. If you were to start with a paved terrace overlooking the sea, with perhaps the protection of some trellis or a low wall, I would invest in several good-sized troughs, at least 16 in. deep and wide, and up to 36

in. long, and plant them up as a shelter belt, using sea buckthorn (*Hippophae rhamnoides*), male and female to ensure orange berries, whose fine, silvery leaves would blend well with the dark, glossy, evergreen foliage and yellowish-green flowers of *Rhamnus alaternus*. At their feet you could place a frill of *Santolina pinnata*, the cotton lavender, its ferny green leaves and creamy flowers providing a solid hedge. You could use some large, wooden tubs for a group of small trees, such as *Crataegus* (hawthorn), whose many interesting cultivars are superb for exposed, windy situations, tolerating even drought and neglect, and growing into gnarled, decorative shapes. A eucalyptus, and one of the hollies of the *Ilex × meserveae* group, together with *Griselinia littoralis*, whose leathery, apple-green leaves would provide good contrast, could complete your background planting.

For color and further interest, you could plant a large terra-cotta pot with a spiky *Cordyline australis*, surrounded by a mass of daisy-flowered arctotis and jewel-colored mesembryanthemums in troughs or low boxes. The broom family (Leguminosae) enjoys coastal life, and grows easily from seed. *Fuchsia magellanica* and other cultivars will provide flowers from summer until autumn; hebes and parahebes, with their enormous range of foliage and flowers, together with *Bupleurum fruticosum* with its sea-green foliage and odd, yellow flowers in late summer, could be combined with feathery tamarix.

Many of the daisy flowers we associate with summer are suitable for coastal life, as are the silver foliage plants, such as artemesias, stachys, senecios, phlomis, olearia, osmanthus, rosemary and lavender. Most salvia cultivars will flourish, and fleshy-leaved plants, such as sedums and sempervivums, thrive. Agapanthus are obviously designed for blending their brilliant blue flowers with the sunlit sea.

ABOVE LEFT *Azaleas require acidic compost and also have a prodigious thirst. If these two needs are met, they will flourish and flower prolifically. Height is provided by placing the pot on top of another, upturned pot.*

ABOVE *Water provides a marvelous backdrop for all plants. In this coastal planting in giant olive jars, the pelargoniums are clipped to follow and extend the lines of the pot. With the argyranthemums at their feet, the planting is kept gloriously simple.*

Growing crops in containers

Fresh tomatoes, and the basil to complement them, are grown in hand-decorated pots. Tomatoes require frequent feeding and watering, and this can be easily controlled in pots to ensure the provision of a good crop.

Almost everyone who has ever used containers has at one time grown a few herbs or some tomatoes in a pot or container. Provided you have enough space and a reasonable amount of sun, it is well worth trying out a much wider range of food plants. The yields from a contained vegetable garden will not feed a hungry family of four, but anything freshly grown is appealing, especially in a town, and growing vegetables and fruit in pots can give you great fun as well as some delicious morsels, while fresh herbs can add interest to your cooking.

Fig trees, peach trees and grape vines can all be grown in large tubs or pots; the dwarf rootstocks for apple trees thrive in large containers, while the new compact cultivars of apple are specifically designed for such treatment. It goes without saying that you

will require compost that is as enriched as possible, and a good layer of organic material should be placed over the drainage crocks. As the season progresses, feed fruit trees with regular and copious amounts of a specific fertilizer. Many annual vegetable crops can be successfully grown in troughs or large pots and anyone interested should study the catalogs of reputable seed merchants for cultivars suitable for pot culture, usually listed separately. Reliable crops include French and runner beans, small, fast-maturing carrots, quick-growing lettuces, peppers, radishes, cucumbers and zucchinis. Sow in troughs the larger, more manageable seeds, such as runner and French beans, and simply thin them out when the seedlings become crowded. Lettuce and radishes can be sown in a seed tray and pricked out into a trough if space is available.

Runner beans can provide surprisingly large crops but you will need to fix some trellis at the back of the trough for support. There are several cucumbers specifically bred for windowsill culture, and they do surprisingly well in a sunny position outdoors, provided you give them prodigious amounts of water, pollinate them by hand, and watch constantly for pests. Zucchinis do best in a large half-barrel of their own, filled with almost solid, well-rotted manure, with a layer of compost on top, and watered copiously; the small, decorative custard marrow thrives on the same treatment.

If you have access to a heated greenhouse, then there is even greater scope for growing tender vegetables. Tomatoes, peppers and aubergines, started under glass and brought outside once there is no danger of frost, produce terrific yields. There are several small-fruited cultivars of tomato, ideal for raising in pots; these include 'Supersweet 100,' with sweet, well-flavored cherry fruit; 'Mini Carol Yellow,' a new F_1 hybrid, which is its yellow counterpart; and 'Red Robin,' easily grown on a sunny windowsill, which offers bunches of bite-sized fruit.

However limited your space, a collection of herbs is almost essential in any container garden. You can

Strawberries do well in the large terra-cotta pots with holes all the way around, from top to bottom, and they are decorative as well as productive; alpine strawberries, in particular, have a most delicious flavor.

plant several herbs together in a trough, a large pot or an old sink or you might consider an herb hanging basket, which will look decorative and give you enough variety to enliven your cooking. Try in it a mix of dark basil (*Ocimum basilicum*), golden-leaved oregano (*Origanum vulgare* 'Aureum'), *Thymus nummularius* and bronze fennel (*Foeniculum vulgare*), with a small French parsley plant slipped in. As with all herbs, they will start to spread and run to seed if not used enough; if space allows, have two or three plants of anything you use regularly, and pick from different plants each time—decimating a basil plant completely is the surest way to kill it off.

Many herbs are decorative enough to plant in isolation. Parsley makes a pretty, frilled edging to pots and boxes and I often plant it all around a shrub or small tree, using small, rooted plants and making sure the soil has been well enriched first. Rosemary will live happily in a sunny position in a pot and benefits from constant nipping out of the tips, becoming bushy and interestingly gnarled with time. Thyme, particularly the golden-leaved cultivar, is an attractive foliage plant in its own right and can be tucked into any sunny, well-drained corner of a container garden, or given a fat pot to itself. The decorative *Origanum* 'Kent Beauty' is one of my favorite container plants, with its ravishing greenish-mauve flowerlets and delicate, veined leaves pouring prettily down the sides of a pot all summer. Lemon balm and mint can be planted in a container but, given their invasive tendencies, may be happier in a raised bed where they can spread.

For all those who like a challenge, this planted vegetable garden demonstrates what can be achieved in containers, from climbing peas and beans to individually planted cauliflowers.

Children's gardens

BELOW *Easily managed pots for children contain marigolds (*Tagetes*), wallflowers and pansies, all colorful, rewarding and readily raised from seeds.*

OPPOSITE *No child could resist these engaging birds perched in their window box of nasturtiums. Both flowers and leaves can be picked for salads.*

Everyone would like their children to have hobbies, preferably ones which keep them quiet and are not wildly anti-social. Gardening fits the bill perfectly, and tending plants in containers often appeals to a child much more than wandering around after a parent pushing a lawn mower. A set of small hand tools, a lightweight watering can and a hand-spray are the only necessities, other than the container and its space. Provided parents take the trouble to make the whole enterprise fun from the start, they are more likely to make garden converts of their children than if they were to hand over a dank, sunless patch in a corner of the garden and expect their child to enjoy it. Obviously someone will have to help with watering, if only by reminding the child, and some form of reward for endeavor, apart from success itself, always helps a great deal.

One of my daughters, deeply prejudiced against all forms of gardening on the grounds that I spent far too much time on it and neglected her, was reluctantly won over by winning the second prize in a window box competition and getting her name in the newspaper at the age of eight. She helped select the window box, plants and seeds and even the compost and drainage material. She enjoyed wandering around our local garden center and chose a dwarf conifer for the center, some pansies, lobelia in strips, petunias in small pots, a packet of trailing nasturtium seeds and a mixed clump of sweet peas.

Children on the whole lack patience, so the "instant" planting of fully grown annuals helps to temper the wait for seeds to emerge from bare earth. Pansies have great allure for children, their engaging faces turned obligingly toward them each morning. My daughter learned early the art of dead-heading, her enthusiasm frequently resulting in a forest of stumpy stalks with not a flower in sight. With practice she improved, however, and the fun of pulling the petunia trumpets out when crumpled only palled when aphids appeared.

Seed planting for children needs to be simple and quick. Not for them the trays, pricking out and final positions routine. They prefer to sow something where it will remain, requiring only thinning out of the seedlings. Morning glory can be placed, several at a time, in a pot, started on an indoor windowsill and watched while they start to climb up the bamboo sticks. *Cobaea scandens* (their cup and saucer flowers perfect for childish tea parties), climbing nasturtiums and black-eyed Susan are all easy and rewarding plants to grow from seed, as are runner beans in the child's vegetable garden.

It is important to teach children some simple propagation too, so they realize that plants do not arrive by magic in the garden center. Most children enjoy placing cuttings in water in a glass jar: they can watch the roots forming, help to disentangle the plantlets, and plant them in compost later on. Fuchsia cuttings always oblige in the glass jar and they are a favorite for their amusing flowers, brightly

Sunflower seeds can be sown in a pot, three or four at a time, to allow for later removal.

colored and easily "popped." The spider plant is also quickly rooted and grows almost as you look at it. If you grow seeds correctly and can transplant seedlings into the child's container garden, let them help if they are at a sensible age; it gives them a sense of continuity and the delicacy of touch required is good practice.

Alpine troughs make a good jumping-off point for children, allowing them to start nose-to-nose and create a miniature landscape for themselves (see page 98). A vegetable garden is also rewarding for children, the crops, however small, being exciting to harvest and a tremendous source of pride when shown to visiting friends (see page 92).

As children get older, their horticultural interests may widen and can still be catered for in containers. Bulbs become appealing, especially dwarf narcissi,

grape hyacinths, small tulips, crocuses, even lilies, as well as the more tactile of shrubs such as the strokeable *Hebe* 'Green Globe,' rosemary and prostrate conifers. You could graduate to a miniature water garden in a low, wide container, provided it has enough depth for a dwarf water lily, aerating plants and a few goldfish, with perhaps a weeping *Salix caprea* in a pot beside it. Even a low, shell-shaped bowl with water inside will attract visiting birds and entertain small as well as older children happily. Add a hanging bird feeder in winter, and the most unpromising roof or balcony can lure children into a lifetime's happy pottering. Even if a child loses interest in gardening for a time, and turns into a plant-hating teenager, bored to tears by such a dreary pastime, the chances are that he or she may well emerge later on as a real gardener.

CONTAINER-FRIENDLY PLANTS FOR CHILDREN

Amaranthus caudatus

Antirrhinum

Bamboos

Campanula pusilla

Cyclamen persicum

Dorotheanthus bellidiformis (mesembryanthemums)

Erigeron aureus

Fuchsia

Lobelia

Mimulus

Myosotis

Nigella

Ophiopogon planiscapus

Papaver (poppies)

Petunia

Sedum

Sempervivum

Silene (campion)

Tropaeolum (nasturtiums)

Viola

Containers for less active gardeners

Container gardening can be designed specifically for gardeners who cannot manage a normal garden, whether for reasons of old age or some form of disability. Many of the vast army of gardeners eventually develop arthritis or even become wheelchair-bound, besides the normal slowing-down process, and it makes sense to do some forward planning to cope with this eventuality. Built-up beds with wider, paved paths in between, slopes rather than steps, alpine sinks on supports, urns on pedestals and waist-high water gardens all make a contribution to manageable and therefore enjoyable gardening for less active people.

Part of a larger garden can be adapted gradually, starting with paths, beds, shelter and easy access, and eventually possibly building on a greenhouse or conservatory, as well as using solid and easily managed containers. Even replacing a demanding lawn with paving or gravel lightens the burden, and installing a self-watering system for pots and raised beds facilitates restricted gardening.

Different forms of handicap will often require different solutions. Blind gardeners must have scent, sound and safety, enhanced with tactile plants such as *Stachys lanata*, hebes and saxifrages. Spiky plants are ruled out, of course, but bamboos, with their rustling leaves, are a useful addition, and the thornless rose, 'Zéphirine Drouhin,' comes into its own. A weeping silver birch makes an excellent container tree, with its branches drooping downward within easy reach.

Wheelchair users require space and leeway at ground level, but can fill window boxes, hanging baskets, troughs and masses of smaller containers set at waist height. Neat alpines, miniature bulbs, bonsai and any amount of seedlings and cuttings could be managed. Tools are now available for longer reach, one-handed work and extra light handling.

The important thing is to choose gentle-natured plants, unlikely to grow too ferociously or be ultrademanding. Select old-fashioned roses, or the patio roses whose pruning requirements are acceptable; put plump box balls into solid pots, choose nonprickly hollies, such as 'J.C. van Tol' or the Japanese *Ilex crenata* cultivars which make neat miniature trees. Artemisias, santolinas, senecios and helianthemums make trouble-free permanent plantings in sun; *Pachysandra terminalis* 'Variegata,' *Euonymus fortunei* 'Emerald Gaiety,' 'Silver Queen' and 'Variegatus' in slight shade.

If the owner can get about but needs frequent rest, provide plenty of seating and build wide edges to any raised beds, on which he or she can perch.

Scented plants for containers

SCENTED PLANTS

Fragrant flowers

Daphne

Hoya

Jasminum

Lilium

Mahonia

Myrtus

Matthiola bicornis

Primula

Stephanotis

Verbena

Viburnum

Aromatic foliage

Eucalyptus

Lavandula

Lippia graveolens

Melissa officinalis

Origanum

Pelargonium

Rosmarinus

Salvia officinale

Santolina

Thymus

One of the many advantages of movable gardens is being able to arrange an especially sweetly scented pot below a window or beside a favorite seat. This is the place for pots of lilies, night-scented stock or heliotropes; you might have bowls of massed balsams (*Impatiens balsamina*) for summer, or Universal Plus pansies for winter cheer, with their delicate, haunting scent; or you could choose a group of scented-leaved pelargoniums, or clumps of *Dianthus* 'Loveliness,' with shaggy flowers of unsurpassed sweetness.

Use the power of scent to cheer up a shady corner: tuck a pot of *Sarcococca* to astonish those who pass by with its secret and magical smell, the more delightful because it is so unexpected. Put a trough filled with skimmias under a north-facing window, and remember to sniff it in late spring. A skimmia makes an excellent shrub to set in a pot by the front door; combine it, perhaps, with a lemon verbena or a rosemary bush, for visitors to touch and smell.

Several climbing plants suitable for containers are scented, but few smell as delectable as *Trachelospermum jasminoides*, the graceful, twining, white-flowered evergreen, perfectly suited to a sheltered porch. Summer-flowering jasmine has a sweet smell and a honeysuckle in a large pot will solve the problem of a shady wall most fragrantly. Many herbs have pleasant-smelling leaves, especially when bruised with the fingers, causing them to release their aromatic properties.

Wallflowers always smell wonderful, as do hyacinths, narcissi and old-fashioned sweet peas. Try growing some sweet peas from seed, then plant them out in very rich compost in a large pot. Instead of training them up a wall, continually pinch out the growing points, allowing them to form a spreading mass covered in sweet-scented flowers.

These handsome pots of Lilium regale and L. rubellum provide instant lift for a corner of the garden, seen against lavender, Nicotiana and the foliage of peonies. Their magical scent will pervade the air around them.

Trying out alpines

Primula auricula
Auriculas, sometimes known as dusty miller for their air of being sprinkled with silvery dust, are well known through botanic paintings. They feature in John Gerard's famous Herbal *of 1597, and were then pounced upon by breeders, becoming ever more stylized. Their stiff elegance, well matched to the fashion in costume of the period, was captured in paint and embroidery.*

Alpine gardens are one of the most distinctive forms of container growing, and indeed sinks and troughs are a very effective way of displaying alpines, many of which are diminutive by nature. As with so many specialist aspects of gardening, the deeper the knowledge, the more enjoyment to be found. Most nurseries or large garden centers have decent alpine corners, but browsing through specialist catalogs will widen the choice of plants. A good deal of excellent advice is available from clubs and specialist magazines. The most important requirement of alpines is good drainage; they must not get damp.

The list of tempting alpine plants is vast, and the number of its devotees vaster, but incorporating these treasures into a true garden is not as easy as it looks. Unless your sink garden is to be a jumble of small plants, some sort of scale has to be introduced. Scale is important in all forms of container gardening but even more vital here. If you are planting alpines in a single container, consider a miniature *Juniperus communis* 'Compressa,' hurtling upward at the rate of ½ in. a year, to introduce solidity and height; use a well-shaped stone to form a fairy's cliff with tiny trailers to hang over the edges; *Linaria alpina* with its snapdragon flowers, purple with orange stripes, all summer; use a dwarf hebe such as *Hebe*

tetrasticha or silvery *H. pinguifolia* to provide bulk.

Try to get a variety of shapes and forms in your trough or sink. Mix cushions and spiky plants with spreaders and trailing species, such as the blue-flowered *Cyananthus microphyllus*; and perhaps sempervivums. If your trough is raised, this landscaping is even more vital, so when embarking on an alpine container, think about the shapes and contrasts, and remember to put in some miniature bulbs for spring.

Where space permits, it can be effective to use an entire terrace or paved area exclusively for alpine containers, some raised on tall stone pedestals, some on low ones and others at ground level. The eye quickly becomes attuned to studying these tiny, delicate masterpieces. The miniature cyclamen, though not strictly alpines, make striking notes with their flyaway, piglet-ears, their delectable variable marbled leaves and their flowers in shades of white or pink. A group of species cyclamen, each in its own low pan, could cluster at the foot of a trough.

Reliable alpine plants

Most of us admire the delicate beauty of alpines: the miraculous finesse of lewisias, gentians, saxifrages, primulas, sedums or auriculas. Among the alpine shrubs suitable for container work are *Ilex crenata*

Planting an alpine trough

Select your plants, with a mixture of shapes, ultimate sizes and flowering times. Choose specially formulated compost if you are buying it, otherwise mix extra-fine grit with your container compost. Before filling the sink or trough, add more drainage material than normal with an additional layer of coarse shingle and omit sod, manure or extra-rich compost. If you are using stones to form a miniature rock garden, half-fill the trough and position them before filling further and finally planting.

Put the plants in firmly but lightly, with the potential trailers around the edges, and the uprights and mound-formers in the middle.

'Mariesii'—a dwarf and very slow-growing holly, good for providing scale and permanency; *Sorbus reducta*, a tiny shrub with finely cut dark, glossy leaves turning bronze and purple in autumn, and pink flowers—it prefers moist, peaty soil, so might be placed in the shade of a "cliff"; *Salix × boydii*, a pretty miniature willow, producing pale yellow catkins in early summer; *Helianthemum alpestre* 'Serpyllifolium,' a low-lying rock rose producing masses of flat, saucer-shaped yellow flowers in summer; *Dianthus alpinus*, making a nice, rounded cushion with fringed pink and white flowers in mid-summer.

The saxifrage family and the sedums provide some of the easiest alpines for beginners. Sedums or stonecrops are colorful, mainly easy, and mat-forming or sprawling, with thick, fleshy leaves, producing abundant starry flowers in mid-summer. *Sedum* 'Coral Carpet' has pretty red leaves and pink flowers, while *S. sieboldii* is trailing and slightly delicate. *Sedum spathuifolium* forms a dense, purple-green mat of spoon-shaped leaves with bright yellow flowers in late spring. *Sedum* 'Ruby Glow' has arching stems of deep purple leaves with dusty pink flowers, and is reliable and successful in pots.

Saxifrages divide into mossy, mound-forming or encrusted (silver) species, with rosettes or leathery, silvery leaves, cushion-forming rosettes or dense hummocks. The best encrusted, or silver, saxifrage for pots is 'Tumbling Waters,' whose large white flowers pour out and down, below the pretty silvery leaves. It prefers repotting at least in alternate years, becoming sulky if left, and failing to flower. *Saxifraga umbrosa*, known as London pride, is a much-loved and reliable, shade-tolerant standby, and *S. umbrosa* 'Primuloides' is like a miniature version, with sprays of bright red to salmon flowers in summer, preferring moist, light shade.

The Auricula group of primulas could be included as an honored part of an alpine garden, their wonderfully artificial, painted flowers on straight, stems rising from stiff, dusty, leathery leaves, better suited to pots than almost any other plant. They enjoy gritty compost and a shady position.

In this, as in all the other forms of enclosed garden we are discussing, ruthlessness is necessary: invasive hummocks must be controlled; spreaders must be frustrated in order to allow gentler treasures the space to breathe. A clump of *Helleborus foetidus* can suddenly stretch its elegant, pointed fingers over whole clumps of starry ramondas. Miniature sisyrinchiums, good for introducing sharp contrast, spread with glee and have to be whisked out severely. In short, discard anything which grows too vigorously, which turns out to be normal size, not miniature, or whose habits are too anti-social.

Keep a watchful eye on bird-sown weeds in your alpine bed—because of the fine grit necessary for alpine health, seeds germinate and grow at astonishing speeds.

A raised bed with alpines growing among well-positioned rocks. All the plants are surrounded by fine grit for good drainage. There is interest all year round, provided by the sedums, Dianthus alpinus, Saxifraga *and dwarf conifer.*

Water gardens

This perfect miniature water garden is created very simply in a stone trough. Planted with a Nymphaea pygmea *'Alba' (a small-sized water lily) and a* Butomus umbellatus, *it makes a focal point in a small courtyard.*

A pond can make a superb decorative feature in the smallest of gardens, and a large fiberglass container, without drainage holes, can easily become a water garden in itself. The position is of course important: too shady a site will prevent aquatic plants from growing, while overhanging deciduous trees will fill the pond with leaves in autumn, causing problems to both fish and plants. A sunny, reasonably sheltered spot is ideal. If you intend putting fish into your pond, at least part of it must be 15 in. deep, to give them adequate protection in the winter.

When it is built—or selected in the case of containers—your water garden needs planting. Oxygenating plants must go in first: they are generally supplied by specialist nurseries in the form of cut stems, which can be placed directly into gravel, or into small pots which can be placed on the bottom. I always put a thin layer of small, rounded pebbles at the bottom of butyl-lined ponds, both to mask their raw newness and to anchor these first oxygenating plants. Among the best of this group are: *Elodea crispa*, *Ranunculus aquatilis*, *Potamogeton crispus*, *Callitriche verna* and *Ceratophyllum dermersum*. The elodeas are really best known to owners of glass-bowled goldfish and they need to be watched; unwatched, they will spread like wildfire over the small container pond.

Once oxygenating plants are established, other aquatic plants can be gradually introduced. One of the best and most reliable flowering water plants is the water hawthorn, *Aponogeton distachyus*, with long, floating green leaves, and sweet-smelling white flowers with black anthers which continue for several months, beginning in mid-summer. Other suitable and attractive water plants include *Menyanthes trifoliata*, with triple green leaves and fringed white flowers in spring, *Pontederia cordata*, producing blue flowers in late summer, and the water hyacinth, *Eichhornia crassipes*, which floats on top of the pond, bearing attractive blue and lilac flowers in summer.

True water lilies are mostly too big for our small space, but *Nymphaea pygmaea helvola*, as its name suggests, is miniature enough, and produces pale yellow flowers about 2 in. across. Plant this in a special aquatic plant pot, in good loam, covering the top with thick gravel if you have fish; it should be raised on bricks at first, and gradually lowered as the leaves grow, until it rests on the bottom. Repotting may become necessary after two or three years.

One of the great joys of even a tiny water garden in your courtyard is the number of birds it entices, and frogs too in many cases. You will almost never see a slug on your plants, and the friendly faces peering from the pond add joy to any tiny town space. Either build your pond with an edging for sitting on, or use a container with a lip, to ensure that birds can perch to drink. Add a bowl or large shell, kept topped up with clean water, and you have a bird-bath-*cum*-water garden which will give you immense pleasure, and delight the birds for miles around. Here too is an excellent position for ornamental fantasies—sculpted

doves, Thai fish, lead lily pads or even lead herons. It is important to keep the water clean, removing fallen leaves and debris promptly. You should also raise the level of water when the skies fail you.

Fountains—either sparkling jets of water or small, bubbling affairs—are a great asset in small gardens, and even more so if the gardener is blind. Provided you have an outdoor electrical outlet, properly installed by an expert, even the smallest pond can have a fountain. Modern, submersible pumps recycle your water, and the only limit to the fun you can have is space and your pocketbook.

Equally attractive in a paved, sunny courtyard, provided it is not visited by very small children, is a sunken water garden, left empty to reflect sky and clouds, offering another dimension to your garden. You could set architectural plants in low containers at the four corners—perhaps agapanthus in blue-glazed Thai pots, or four stylish standard Portuguese laurel (*Prunus lusitanica*).

Hostas are superb in containers, and yours can be placed at the base of the water garden, with their leaves arching over it, perhaps with some astilbes alongside: both are excellent pot subjects with a liking for water. Not only do they have a close affinity with ponds and water gardens, but they are both thirsty plants and require generous amounts of water to drink. The decorative umbrella plant (*Cyperus involucratus*) can be stood in the pond during mild weather, providing grace and height.

A marvelous dimension is added to this garden in the form of a rectangular pond with a paved surround. Here the well-positioned pots combine with a superbly mossed Ali Baba jar to create a sense of peace.

101

THROUGH
THE SEASONS

As with most undertakings, keeping things going after the initial rush of enthusiasm is the hardest part about container gardening. It is easy to plant up your tubs joyfully when spring rustles and burgeons, and to water and feed them in summer when they are frothy and flowery. The tricky bit is maintaining the impetus with all your pots during the months when everything is dank and soggy. You should plan in one season for improving another, always looking ahead hopefully and backward critically. This section will act as your adviser, reminder and conscience.

Every season has its own particular appeal, and when planting your containers it is important to remember the glorious range of autumn leaf coloring. This Japanese maple (Acer palmatum 'Dissectum Atropurpureum'), a delectable shade of raspberry and then plum-purple all summer, flames vigorously when the early leaves start falling, continuing until the first frost arrives.

Spring

The first glimpse of a pale, low spring sun, promising glimpses of fresh green, will send you rushing outside to check on progress and speed things up. One of the greatest temptations is to cut and snip too soon, forcing delicate young foliage out, only to face icy winds or late frosts. Restrain yourself in early spring to enjoying snowdrops, crocus or chionodoxa, and looking out for the thick buds of all your early-flowering *Narcissus*. Any winter-flowering jasmine will still be throwing its golden stars against a wall, and bergenias, pulmonarias and hellebores will all be beginning to flower, while *Mahonia japonica* still fills the garden with its deliciously scented yellow racemes. When it has finished, cut it back in the knowledge that new shoots will rush forth to cover the yellow wound.

Helleborus foetidus, *H. argutifolius* and *H. viridis* survive well in raised beds or large pots, seeding themselves prolifically in every available cranny; their elegant, pale green flowers and architectural leaves are a perfect foil to the yellows, blues and whites of spring. *Pulmonaria* 'Sissinghurst White' has a mass of small, white trumpet-flowers borne well above the pointed spotted leaves. *Bergenia* 'Silberlicht' holds pure white flowers, occasionally pink-tinged, clear of its rounded, leathery, evergreen leaves. These two plants, combined with *Dicentra spectabilis* 'Alba,' planted at the foot of a spring-flowering camellia with an evergreen fern and some hostas, would provide a good north-facing spring composition, requiring only plenty of autumn mulching and an early-spring feed.

If your garden is larger, containers forming but a part of it, your spring bedding schemes will be well advanced, and you could have pots of grape hyacinths, scillas, polyanthus, or hyacinths drowning you with scent, and troughs of fat-budded tulips to follow on.

Pot-grown Narcissus *'Tête-à-tête' added to* Cordyline australis *and* Hedera helix *'Glacier.'*

Treat time

If this is your first gardening season, or autumn caught you unaware, or indeed if your space is too tiny to allow for any forward planning, now is the moment to start a well-orchestrated series of treats. Most nurseries or garden centers have trays of early-flowering bulbs just about to burst out; they also have forced polyanthus, primulas, dwarf iris and other delights. Plant a pot or pots, clearly visible from your sitting room or kitchen window, and gaze at them, allowing their bright color to fill you with spring cheer. Polyanthus, provided the birds do not pick off the flowers, will continue flowering for four to six weeks, and narcissi for as long if kept well dead-headed. An early-spring window box can be created in this way. Besides inspiring us, spring brings a good many chores along with it.

- Inspect all your pots, troughs, raised beds or boxes. Remove any forms of winter protection and repair any frost-damaged containers, then look at the plants. However much you tidied and pruned in the autumn, more will need to be done. In large, mixed plantings, remove some of the topsoil, making holes in the root mass and down the sides of containers with a sharp stick, and force as much fresh compost, mixed with general fertilizer, into the gaps as you can. Do any root pruning you may feel necessary.
- Lift and divide any perennials, particularly trailers such as ivy, whose foliage looks too woody. Remove them from the pot, throw out the woody center of the plant, and replant the outer growths, cutting back any too-long shoots. I am always tempted to leave a composition which looks happy, but boldness generally pays off; most constricted plants repay thinning, repotting or re-arranging with renewed vigor.
- Such precious shrubs as the Japanese maples need repotting about every third year, or at least a compost replacement.
- *Climbers* Spring-flowering clematis, such as *C. macropetala* and *C. alpina*, should be lightly cut back after flowering, to make space for their new tendrils. Delicate climbers, such as *Solanum jasminoides* 'Album,' should be left until late spring, and only then have any dead bits cut back. *Solanum crispum* should be cut back quite severely in spring, to prevent it smothering you; *S. crispum* 'Glasnevin' is hardier, less invasive and flowers for longer but, ideally, should be cut back a little in early spring, and any dead shoots removed entirely.

Add extra wall nails and wire, and strengthen existing wires or trellis if necessary. Cut back the spent flowering trails of *Clematis armandii* and train in its long, winding new shoots.

- Prune roses, feeding with brand-name rose

fertilizer as you do so. If mildew and black spot were particularly rampant the previous year, try and take preventative measures earlier in the season.

● Give all containers a thorough drenching, particularly the most thickly planted ones. This might sound obvious, but when it is raining outside, it is tempting to forego this chore. If you have several pots on a paved terrace, first water all round, then start at the beginning and go round them again, checking at the end that a good amount of water has come through the drainage holes onto the paving—sometimes a third journey becomes necessary for the first onslaught of the year.

● Wash down evergreens with plenty of clean water, thoroughly cleaning up any particularly pollution-tinged plants. Inspect them for soot, or sticky signs of caterpillar and grub infestation, and spray with a suitable early-prevention treatment.

● Sow any annuals, perennials, shrubs, trees or climbers that you intend to grow from seed and plant out any rooted cuttings you have been nurturing, or young plants over-wintered under glass.

● Remove old soil from window boxes for which you plan a complete spring display. If you replanted the boxes in autumn with bulbs underneath winter evergreens, this can be postponed until after their flowering is over.

● Plant any summer-flowering bulbs or corms, such as gladioli, dahlias, alliums or lilies, and remember to make a note of what has gone where. It is wise, if you have a number of containers, to keep a record of what you plant, when you plant it, and how it does, both to help improve your choice and to avoid repeating a failure. A garden diary helps here, if only to prevent burying expensive lilies beneath unsuitable companions.

This superb summer planting uses lush and varied foliage and restrained color.

Summer

In container gardening, summer is generally considered the most important of all the seasons; indeed, many people only think about their pots and boxes when the sun is shining. Window boxes and hanging baskets are an essential component of our vision of a potted garden and one reason for this is our use of half-hardy and tender bedding plants to provide maximum color and impact. Who can picture a well-designed urn without petunias, pelargoniums, lobelias or Paris daisies (*Argyranthemum frutescens*)? To achieve this perfection, we must plant well, maintain superbly and be ruthless with recalcitrant plantings. Summer is a busy season for maintenance.

Top of the list of requirements comes watering—too many potentially attractive schemes come to grief because no one remembers to water them often enough. The drying summer sun may well produce superb blooms but it can also kill plants off totally, and most bedding and foliage plants are unforgiving of neglect. Only pelargoniums and mesembryanthemums will withstand drying out.

Hostas, Japanese maples, and hydrangeas in shaded containers are at their best in mid-summer; the invaluable *Impatiens* provide color amongst them, as do begonias, astilbes and day lilies. Roses, if you have large enough raised beds, are superb now; jasmines, honeysuckles, trachelospermum, morning glory, *Cobaea scandens*, bougainvillea, passion flower, plumbago and wisteria are covering walls and trellis; all the daisy family, the pelargoniums, the salvias, as well as heucheras, fuchsias, verbenas, petunias and hebes are flowering away cheerfully. Lilies fill the garden with their swooning scent, and buddlejas attract a variety of butterflies.

● The chore list for summer is somewhat repetitive—water, dead-head and feed, on and on, each day for many containers, and twice a day for hanging baskets in full sun—unless, of course, you had the foresight to install a self-watering system. Before you depart on vacation, line up a friend for the watering and remove all visible flowers to ensure you have something to come home to.

● Stake anything that is threatening to flop. Short bamboos can be pushed in behind almost anything, particularly roses, hebes, pittosporums or fuchsias, whose growth is falling too far forward. Tie some of the flopping stems lightly to the stake, thus pulling the whole plant into line. The same technique can be used to keep climbers in place, and to stretch a group of annuals to cover a gap or banish an invasive shrub trying to smother the bedding plants. If your urn lacks height in the middle, a bamboo can be used to train a *Helichrysum petiolare* or a fuchsia upward, to form a pillar. Treat ivies similarly, or any other trailing or climbing plant, such as morning glory or nasturtiums.

• Lightly prune or cut back any early-flowering shrubs such as ceanothus, viburnums and camellias, as well as early perennials such as campanulas, aubrietas and candytufts (*Iberis*).

• When roses start to fade, cut the spray back to a pair of sturdy-looking leaves, or pick a good branch for the house, thus pruning as you go. Keep using foliage plants such as pittosporums, viburnums, eucalyptus or rhamnus for indoor flower arrangements. Snip off bits of herbs and rosemary regularly, to keep the plants bushy. Toward late summer, cut back violas and feed, to encourage a second flowering.

• Put a weak solution of suitable foliar feed into the watering can once a week. Give camellias, azaleas and rhododendrons a dose of brand-name acidic plant food after flowering, before the end of the summer.

• Check your plants every few days for pests and diseases and apply suitable organic remedies. You will need to wage constant battle against aphids, in particular, but well-fed and well-watered plants are less likely to succumb to invasions of aphids.

• Water gardens need watching for too-invasive aerating plants, which threaten to swamp everything. Keep small ponds filled, as evaporation works swiftly in the summer months. Remember to fill a bowl or large shell for birds to drink from if your pond is deep—and top it up regularly.

• Sow any biennials you need, such as campanulas, lupins or Sweet Williams. Take cuttings of any shrubs or half-hardy sub-shrubs toward the end of summer, if you have space to bring them on.

• Continue to train standards or topiary specimens, foliar feeding as you go.

The shade of an antique "copper" enhances a fading, autumnal Hydrangea macrophylla.

Autumn

This season has many devotees due to the glorious mixture of autumn colors produced by trees and shrubs as well as the the soft days with crisp mornings. Japanese maples light up a corner with their brilliant flames; *Vitis coignetiae* turns its huge, flat leaves to magnificent crimson and orange plates; hostas go from green to gold overnight. Birches, sorbus, *Rhus typhina*, azaleas, cornus, vaccinium, various prunus, and ceratostigma, all provide an important color statement lasting far into the season.

This is a time for reviewing the performance of your container garden. Check each pot with a critical eye; did it perform as you planned? If not, what went wrong, and can you remedy it? If a shrub or tree has outgrown its allotted space, despite pruning, and is too large to re-pot, replant it in the garden or find a friend to give it to. Autumn is also the season for planting new shrubs and trees. If your taste has changed during the year, or you have admired a particular plant, now is the best time to order it from a nursery. If you garden in a mild area, evergreens can also be planted now; if not, wait until spring. Give a newcomer fresh compost and plenty of water to start it off.

• Clean and tidy your container garden thoroughly, removing all dead flowers and foliage. Small and city gardens should *always* be immaculate; a billowing effect must not preclude hygiene. If you have a spare corner, fill some polyethylene bags with leaves, put in a brand-name compost-maker, make some holes in the bag, tie it up and leave it to make valuable leaf mold.

• Plant any spring-flowering bulbs, using the three-tier method in window boxes (see page 25), and also any spring-flowering biennials such as wallflowers, foxgloves or honesty in shaded corners.

• Firmly tie climbing roses, including any newly pruned climbers, to walls or trellis, remembering the ferocity of winter winds. Check the trellis on a balcony or roof for the same reason, and inspect trees and their stakes; cut back the branches of any trees whose top growth looks too risky. Ceanothus, particularly, has a habit of putting on tremendous growth during the summer, and becoming quite top-heavy by the autumn.

• Spring-flowering perennials can be divided now. Lily of the valley and hostas can be split up and replanted in fresh compost and bracken ferns lifted and spread around, provided the soil is still quite warm.

• Arrange protection for delicate specimens, such as *Melianthus major*, standard argyranthemums, fuchsias, heliotropes or felicias, either by moving them into a conservatory or rigging up some form of barrier or shelter (see page 36–37).

- Mulch where possible, with a good layer of manure. Give pot-grown lilies a generous mulch of leaf mold or cut bracken fern.
- In some areas, birds create havoc amongst mulched pots in spring, and a covering of bark chippings or gravel is vital. Where a pot holds a self-seeding plant, such as a hellebore, a mulch of gravel acts as an effective seed medium, and will allow sturdy seedlings to develop in due course.
- It is tempting if the weather is gloomy to retreat indoors in autumn. But remember the joy spring bulbs gave you and how splendid the pots of tulips looked with the sun on them, then rush out and plant some before it freezes. If your larger containers are still looking too good to disband, put the tulips in a large plastic pot, which can be lowered into a terra-cotta one in spring, or even put them into a decorative basket just before flowering. This principle can be applied to lilies and any spring bulbs that are better massed together, such as narcissi, hyacinths or crocus; set the plastic pots in a corner or position them behind an ornamental pot, to await their turn on stage.
- Remove fallen leaves from pots or beds, and prevent any falling into the pond. Cut off any dead branches or twigs from shrubs and trees, and tweak out dead annuals from all the containers.
- Inspect any conifers carefully. Some, such as *Cupressus glabra*, have a tendency to die off in the center, producing brownish dead foliage, which should be removed whenever it is spotted. Cut it back to a healthy branch or twig. If the tree is thick, open its center and make sure no dead bits are lurking inside. Any *Cupressus* which have been used as backing or windbreak trees in, for instance, a raised bed, can have their lower branches removed, turning them into standards, to allow more space for shrubs at their feet.

Frost-painted branches and a cascade of ivy brighten the frozen winter landscape.

Winter

No container gardener should overlook winter. So many city gardeners close the curtains and switch on the lights, the better to read gardening books and shrub catalogs. But if you plan a backdrop of evergreens or foliage plants, you will still have something to enjoy from your windows. Ligustrum, pittosporum, rhamnus, *Viburnum tinus*, *Phormium tenax* and ivy still look handsome. The winter season is also enhanced by hollies (*Ilex*) in all their varied guises as well as choisya, Daphne, skimmia, camellia and *Arbutus unedo*, not to mention box, topiarized or free growing, and the city standby of sweet bay (*Laurus nobilis*).

Even a small window box can contain a pair of miniature cypresses, or a variegated box, with one of the many small-leaved hebes and some ivy to complete the scene.

The Japanese maples, once they have lost their autumn foliage, form wonderful gnarled shapes, best seen against a pale background. Birch trees, upright or weeping, show up well against the pale winter sky. The somber tones of *Ophiopogon planiscapus* 'Nigrescens,' *Phormium tenax* 'Bronze Baby' or *Heuchera* 'Palace Purple,' with possibly *Ajuga reptans* 'Atropurpurea' at their feet, would make a pleasing winter scene, with *Helleborus foetidus* nearby.

- Looking ahead is a popular winter occupation. Order spring-flowering bulbs, and any new shrubs, climbers, trees or roses.
- Plan any improvements to your terrace, roof or balcony, such as outdoor lighting, better trellis, proper walls, or the addition of a water garden or a gazebo. It is wise to arrange such "hard landscape" projects now, weather permitting, before the specialists become swamped by spring clients.
- Keep an eye on your containers, and water them where flagging plants indicate a need; never assume that enough rain falls in winter.
- Move some of the containers around, so that evergreens, conifers or handsome foliage plants come to the fore.
- In very cold weather, huddle your containers together in groups for added protection against frost, and spread a thick layer of bark chippings over any semi-tender subjects. Remember that the walls of a house throw off warmth, and setting standard fuchsias, for instance, against a side wall, with plenty of peat moss-type mulching in the pot, and grouped with tougher subjects in front of them, will give them a better chance if they cannot be taken inside.
- If you have a frost-free shed or conservatory, you will of course bring any vulnerable plants indoors during the most severe months, but failing that you could rig up a "winter overcoat" for them with chicken wire and bracken fern, as shown on page 37.

KEY PLANTS FOR CONTAINER GARDENS

Every gardener has his or her favorite plants and among them will be those which have proved successful and some which remain a challenge. Here I discuss only plants I have used in container work, and know to be willing to thrive under this set of rules. Many of the plant families have other pleasing cultivars, but where I have described only one or two, those featured are the ones I can vouch for in a contained situation. The height and spread given are for plants grown normally, unless specified otherwise. Remember that containers limit growth.

Planting in containers throws the beauty of individual plants into sharp focus. Here, the pink variegated leaves of a Begonia rex *subtly echo the flowers of a dark-leaved zonal* Pelargonium, *their delicacy offset by the rustic, solid stone trough.*

Trees and shrubs

Acer palmatum
'Dissectum Atropurpureum'
(Japanese maple)
The Japanese maples are invaluable for container work, with their elegant form, slow growth and superb foliage.

Trees and shrubs form the backbone of a container garden, whether they are grown for their strong outline, their decorative foliage or simply as an evergreen backdrop for seasonal plantings.

Brugmansia arborea

This cultivar unfurls its bright raspberry-colored leaves in late spring, and they remain marvelously fresh and delicate until they become a flaming bush of many colors in autumn. The winter shape, with its finely etched twigs, has great appeal, especially against gravel or pale walls. Its only insistence is upon plenty of water and a position sheltered from bright sun, which burns the leaves. Its mature bronze-red leaves require careful siting, with preferably an echo of similar coloring within reach; such a graceful, stylish shape also calls for a special container. With its spreading habit, this cultivar may eventually become too wide for a small area, but not for many years.
Size H: to 4 ft.; S: to 5 ft. **Aspect** Tolerates shade. **Planting partners** *Pleioblastus viridistrata* (bamboo, smaller cultivars), *Hosta, Berberis* 'Rose Glow,' *Clematis* 'Hagley Hybrid,' *Fatsia japonica, Camellia, Choisya ternata, Fuchsia, Pieris* 'Forest Flame,' *Pieris japonica* 'Variegata,' *Rhododendron* (azaleas).

Arundinaria viridistrata see
Pleioblastus viridistrata

Brugmansia
syn. *Datura*
(Angel's trumpet)
These large shrubs or small trees, evergreen to semi-evergreen, are grown as spectacular ornaments for sheltered, sunny positions and would make an exotic addition to a sheltered courtyard. Their dramatic flowers hang, trumpet-shaped and showy, from rounded, bushy plants whose large leaves, although somewhat coarse, contribute to the imposing whole. Different cultivars produce white, yellow, pink or red and yellow flowers, and both they and their seeds are poisonous, rendering them unsuitable for a garden with small children around. *B. candida* has strongly scented, dangling white flowers; *B. sanguinea* sports orange-red and yellow trumpets against lobed leaves. They all need generous watering all summer, with weekly feeds from early spring to early autumn, and should be cut back hard in early spring to encourage bushy growth. Propagate by seed in spring, or by cuttings in summer onward. These plants are attractive to whitefly and red spider mite.
Size H and S: to 10 ft., but less when contained and cut back regularly. **Aspect** Requires a frost-free (but light) position in winter and half-shade in summer. **Planting partners** Best alone.

Camellia
The handsome, shiny leaves of these superb evergreen shrubs add style and strength to any group and their flowers are quite unbeatable. There are so many that one can be found for all schemes, from early-flowering to late. Apart from their dislike of drying out at all times, they are the easiest of plants, surviving and even flowering in dauntingly unpromising places. They

benefit from spraying of the leaves in dusty positions and you should feed them well, with bonemeal in autumn and a mulch of old manure, leaf mold or good lime-free compost in spring. No pruning is necessary, but quite drastic cutting back can be done.

The cultivars *C. × williamsii* flower early, and the blooms are shed as they fade. Other particularly decorative cultivars include: *C.* 'Mrs. W. W. Davies,' with delicate, palest pink flowers having pronounced yellow centers; *C.* 'Donation,' with semi-double, large, silvery pink flowers; *C. japonica* 'Contessa Lavinia Maggi,' a formal, double, white flower, streaked with pink; *C. japonica* 'Alba Simplex' or 'White Swan.' *C.* 'Lady Clare' has the advantage of producing a wide, weeping outline and is therefore good for siting in a raised bed or where it will overhang water.

Size H: 6–8 ft.; S: 4–6 ft. **Aspect** Needs shelter from morning sun. **Soil** Requires acidic compost. **Planting partners** All spring and early summer bulbs, *Hosta, Dicentra eximia* and *D. spectabilis, Digitalis* (foxgloves), ferns, *Cyclamen neapolitanum, Polyanthus, Astilbe.*

Ceanothus
'A. T. Johnson'

I often use ceanothus as evergreen backing for large troughs or pots, allowing them to remain for some years, pruning them lightly, and whisking them away to a larger garden when they become overgrown. The bright blue flowers of this vigorous plant are borne freely in late spring to early summer and generally again in autumn. Pruning and shaping is best done after the first flowering, shortening quite ruthlessly if necessary, and removing entire branches where space dictates. This cultivar will allow itself to be trained as a hedge or close-clipped topiary arch, although the flowering may be reduced. Plant in early autumn or late spring; it is easy to root from cuttings taken in mid-summer and then over-wintered in a sheltered frame or greenhouse.

Size H: 5 ft.; S: 10 ft. **Aspect** Prefers full sun and a sheltered position. **Planting partners** *Solanum jasminoides* 'Album,' *Trachelospermum jasminoides, Rhodochiton,* some of the less vigorous *Clematis, Ipomoea hederacea* (morning glory), *Jasminum revolutum, Rosa* 'Aloha,' *Ceratostigma willmottianum.*

Choisya ternata
(Mexican orange)

One of the most valuable evergreen container shrubs, with its aromatic, glossy, hand-shaped leaves and scented white flowers in spring, reappearing at intervals throughout summer. The leaves seem to reflect light, giving the plant a lively, charming air and carrying many different shades of green, making this a satisfying sight in all seasons. A good-sized container, perhaps a solid stone one in classic shape, planted with a well-grown choisya, is a garden in itself. Wide troughs, with choisya growing against the wall, underplanted with spring bulbs and hardy fuchsias for summer,

Camellia 'Inspiration'

make a superb, trouble-free container garden for a busy person. It refurbishes itself from even deep pruning cuts and can be placed almost anywhere; in poor light, it may grow leggy, requiring more pruning and feeding to remain handsome. It is easy to grow from cuttings taken in late summer.

The brilliant golden-leaved 'Sundance' combines well with blue, such as *Ruta graveolens* (rue) or *Eucalyptus gunnii,* or could be toned down with a yew hedge behind. The decorative, finely cut 'Aztec Pearl' is useful where a less solid outline is needed.

Size H and S: 6½–10 ft. **Aspect** Prefers a warm, sunny corner but accepts semi-shade happily and tolerates even deep shade. **Planting partners** *Jasminum nudiflorum, Camellia, Clematis armandii, Solanum jasminoides* 'Album,' *Lilium, Tulipa, Carex morrowii, Ruta graveolens, Eucalyptus gunnii.*

Daphne odora
'Aureomarginata'

Yuccas and New Zealand flax, *Phormium tenax*, provide the same architectural note but are both more permanent and "serious" plants, whereas cordylines are exotic. They are so valuable that container buffs will risk losing them each winter. These evergreen shrubs can also be treated as bedding plants.

'Lentiginosa' or 'Atropurpurea' has purple leaves and provides an effective note against stone or white walls. **Size in container** H: 2–3 ft.; S: 3–4 ft. **Aspect** Enjoys full sun or slight shade. **Planting partners** All the bedding plants: *Pelargonium*, *Viola*, *Petunia*, *Verbena*, *Campanula*, *Felicia*, *Convolvulus mauritanicus*, *Helichrysum petiolare*.

Cordyline australis

These spiky evergreen shrubs have a superb architectural outline. It is worth selecting their container carefully, in a restricted space, as their style demands a well-thought-out scheme. In the center of a large pot they make an excellent foil to balance soft masses of annuals, and they give a good height accent in window boxes, urns or chimney pots, requiring only to be balanced by billowers at their feet. Their spikes throw elegant shadows over paving, providing another dimension. In mild areas and sheltered conditions cordylines grow apace, and stand up to wind, particularly maritime, remarkably well, but they crumple and rot when subjected to frost or severe cold. Suckers from the main plant can be detached in spring and grown on for use the following year.

Coronilla glauca
'Variegata'

This pretty, bushy, evergreen shrub has decorative, blue-gray foliage, with creamy white markings. Its masses of scented, pea-like yellow flowers appear in mid-spring and continue intermittently throughout the summer. It is a suitable shrub to grow against a warm wall or could be treated as a climber. **Size** H and S: 5 ft.; **Aspect** Requires sun and shelter. **Planting partners** *Trachelospermum jasminoides*, *Ruta graveolens*, *Rosmarinus officinalis*, *Thymus* 'Aurea,' *Osteospermum* 'Sunny Boy' or 'Sunny Girl,' *Muscari*, early *Narcissus*.

Crab apple see *Malus*

Daphne odora
'Aureomarginata'

This charming, bushy evergreen shrub has narrow, shiny mid-green leaves with bright golden margins; it produces pale purple flowers with a wonderfully sweet scent in profusion from early spring for one or two months. Its neat shape and size provide a perfect middle plant for a raised bed; any spreading branches can be pruned back by picking bouquets for the house. It can be grown from seed, or from cuttings in late summer. **Size** H and S: to 5 ft. **Aspect** Prefers a sunny position. **Planting partners** *Clematis alpina*, *Helleborus lividus*, *Viola labradorica*, *Saxifraga*, *Fuchsia*, *Erigeron mucronatus*.

Datura see *Brugmansia*

Fatsia japonica
(Japanese Fatsia)

This sculptured, evergreen shrub, with its enormous spreading, hand-shaped leaves and strange, greenish-white flowers in autumn or winter, is invaluable for city gardens. Even in an awkward, dark yard it will stretch out its shiny foliage. The variegated cultivar has creamy white edging and is less vigorous. Pruning is only required when plants grow too large or lanky from poor light, but it will refurbish itself cheerfully. Propagate from seeds sown in late spring or from sucker shoots used as cuttings. **Size** H and S: 10 ft. **Aspect** Tolerates almost any conditions, but prefers shelter from cold winds; in cold areas provide a south or west wall for protection. **Planting partners** Best set alone in a good-sized pot, with clipped variegated ivy (*Hedera*) to dangle, or as a background to bright *Impatiens* in a shady situation. It makes a particularly good contrast for *Arundinaria* (bamboo), *Acer palmatum* (dwarf maple) and *Rhododendron*.

Hebe

This group of slightly tender evergreen shrubs contains a large number of appealing cultivars. Hebes are largely restricted to the less humid West Coast climates. Their wide variety in foliage coloring, shape and growth, their neat habit and cheerful acceptance of severe pruning and transplanting, combined with their length of flowering time and pretty coloring, makes them one of the best plant families for containers. Among my favorite hebes are: *H. rakaiensis*, with dense, glossy olive-green leaves and white flowers in mid-summer; forms a rounded, strokable shape that makes a perfect foil for spiky plants; likes sun. *H. × andersonii* 'Variegata,' a tender shrub with wavy, cream-variegated leaves and lavender flowers from summer till autumn; invaluable as winter bedding, mixed with winter-flowering pansies and trailing ivies. *H.* 'Bowles' Hybrid,' whose mid-green leaves turn a mahogany purple, with deep mauve flowers from late spring till mid-winter, tolerates severe pruning and constant picking. *H. pinguifolia* 'Pagei,' hardy and bushy, with blue-green foliage and small white

flowers freely borne in early summer; its bluish mound makes a good foil for pinks, reds and blues as well as yellows and pure purple. A useful candidate for the front of raised beds. *H. hulkeana*, one of the finest hebes, with glossy green leaves and long, lavender-blue flowers in summer, is good against a sheltered wall.

Size H: 6 in.–4.5 ft.; S: 16 in.–4.5 ft. **Aspect** Prefers sun. **Planting partners** *Phormium tenax* 'Yellow Wave,' yellow daisies, *Salvia farinacea* 'Victoria,' *Teucrium fruticans*, spring bulbs.

Japanese maple see *Acer palmatum*

Japanese pittosporum see **Pittosporum tobira**

Ligustrum
(Privet)

These shrubs become special, indeed invaluable, in containers and are particularly decorative to look down upon. All are easy to root from cuttings, which makes them an excellent, cheap form of evergreen bulk for a mixed raised bed.

L. lucidum is an evergreen tree producing creamy white flowers against glossy dark green oval leaves in summer. *L. lucidum* 'Excelsum Superbum,' with broad leaves edged with yellow, is an excellent permanent container dweller, fresh and handsome all year round, and surviving life on a town roof. *L. lucidum* 'Tricolor' forms an enchanting small tree, its gracefully

Fatsia japonica

arching gray-green leaves pink-tinged on new growth; it is perfect for the container garden needing one small tree to add height to lower plantings.

L. ovalifolium 'Aureomarginatum' makes a tough, cheerful background shrub, with yellow edging; its cultivar 'Variegatum' edges the glossy, mid-green leaves with paler yellow or cream. Both occasionally lose their leaves in hard winters but refurnish in spring. A group of three or five golden privets will brighten a dark corner with glee.

Size H and S: 20 ft. but much less in containers. **Aspect** Tolerates shade. **Planting partners** *Eucalyptus gunnii* against golden privets, *Camellia* against variegated ones, *Anemone × hybrida* 'Louise Uhink,' *Galanthus* (snowdrops), *Narcissus* 'February Gold.'

Magnolia stellata
(Star magnolia)

This elegant, deciduous tree is unusual enough in tubs to lend an air of distinction to your container garden. It is a slow-growing mutant of another, larger cultivar and its pale, soft green leaves follow the strongly scented, star-shaped white flowers which appear in early spring. If early frost or heavy rain spoil the early flowers, they are speedily replaced with a second crop. The cultivar 'Rosea' has pink flowers and a form named 'Water Lily' has larger, thicker flowers. Plant in a good-sized tub and feed annually, but refrain from moving as it resents disturbance.
Size H and S: to 6 ft. **Aspect** Prefers sun; position out of north and east winds. **Soil** Prefers rich, slightly acid compost; keep it moist but free-draining. **Planting partners** Mass small pots of early-spring bulbs at the foot of your tub, followed by a well-grown

Magnolia stellata

fern, *Acer japonicum*, *Acer palmatum*, evergreen *Rhododendron* (azalea) or small *Hosta*.

Malus
'Profusion'
(Crab apple)

This flowering tree, with bronze-green young leaves, can be grown as a small standard in a large wooden tub and will remain a delicate and handsome focal point. It produces masses of deep red buds in spring, which give way to reddish purple flowers with pale pink centers, followed by small, egg-shaped red fruits. Its branches have a handsome, knobbly outline in winter, which looks good against the sky. The tree does not resent pruning or tidying; none is usually required. After a few years the roots may need pruning.
Size H: 15–20 ft.; **S:** 8–15 ft. (but far less in captivity). **Aspect** Prefers sun.
Planting partners *Viola labradorica* 'Purpurea' could be massed at the feet of your tub.

Mexican orange see *Choisya ternata*

Nandina domestica
(Chinese sacred bamboo)

This delicate, half-hardy evergreen shrub has a great affinity with containers; placed in a decorative glazed pot from the East, it creates a stylish and pleasing effect. While it resembles bamboo, the pale green, prettily shaped leaves turn an attractive purplish shade in autumn and are touched with red when young. This handsome

foliage shrub looks best alone, in a good container and seen against a plain background. It produces wide, white panicles in summer which may be followed by white or scarlet fruits lasting into winter. Several cultivars, differing in height, are available.
Size H and S: 12 in.–6 ft. **Aspect** Tolerates quite low light levels, but requires sun to color it for autumn. **Planting partners** None (see above).

Phygelius aequalis
'Yellow Trumpet'

An evergreen sub-shrub with decorative creamy yellow trumpet flowers from mid-summer till autumn. Planted in a good-sized pot, it strikes an exotic note for a sheltered terrace or could form the centerpiece for a sunny courtyard in shades of yellow, white and green. It can be grown from seed, over-wintered in a frame or greenhouse and planted out in position the following year.
Size H and S: 5 ft. **Aspect** Needs sun. **Planting partners** *Felicia amelloides*, *Ipomoea hederacea* (morning glory), *Vinca minor*.

Pieris

This shrub makes an excellent permanent container plant if treated well and watered regularly. The young leaves in spring are a marvelous shrimp-pink, turning dark, gleaming green; the flowers last for several weeks in spring. 'Bert Chandler' has salmon-pink early foliage, turning cream and then white before ending glossy green. 'Forest Flame' has brilliant red young leaves, turning pink and then white. 'Purity' has pure white flowers and 'Blush' shell-pink. *Pieris japonica*, rounded, bushy and dense; young foliage bronze turning to dark green. White flowers in spring; *P. japonica* 'Variegata' is slow-growing. Hardy. Plant in early autumn or spring, in a position sheltered from cold winds; propagate from cuttings taken in late summer. Mulch annually with leaf mold, and feed with brand-name acidic liquid compound. **Size** H and S: 6–11½ ft. **Aspect** Tolerates some degree of shade, provided it is sheltered. **Soil** Use acidic compost. **Planting partners** Has an excellent affinity with other plants from Japan.

Pittosporum tobira
(Japanese pittosporum)

This evergreen shrub or small tree maintains its cheerful air all year round; it forms a bushy outline and responds to severe pruning without resentment. It produces wonderfully sweet-scented flowers in late spring; they last for several months, starting white and deepening to cream, and are shown off to perfection by the shiny, leathery leaves which are more olive than bottle-green, providing another shade to vary the green spectrum. It can form a splendid wall shrub through which to train a delicate climber. 'Variegatum' has pretty silver markings and is less vigorous. **Size** H: 8–13 ft.; S: 6–10 ft., but root restriction would reduce this. **Aspect** A sheltered, sunny position is preferred. **Planting partners** *Solanum jas-*

minoides, *Cobaea scandens*, *Humulus lupus* 'Aureum,' *Phygelius aquaelis* 'Yellow Trumpet,' *Kniphofia* 'Little Maid,' *Osteospermum* 'Buttermilk,' *Phormium tenax* 'Yellow Wave,' *Argyranthemum* 'Jamaica Primrose,' *Zinnia* 'Envy,' *Liriope muscari* 'Variegata,' *Viola cornuta*.

Pleioblastus viridistrata
(formerly *Arundinaria viridistrata*)

This slow-growing, evergreen bamboo has purple stems and bright yellow, green-striped leaves. It is a very good plant to set in a dull corner of a raised bed, where it will spread gently. It responds to severe cutting back in spring by refurnishing itself with new, brighter growth; it is also easy to divide. It should never be allowed to dry out.
Size H: to 5 ft. but less in captivity; S: indefinite. **Aspect** Prefers sun but grows well enough in shade. **Planting partners** *Hedera helix* 'Buttercup,' *Melianthus major*, blue-green *Hosta*, *Campanula*.

Rhamnus alaternus
'Argenteovariegata'

A fast-growing evergreen shrub, eventually a small tree, with charming, small, variegated leaves. It provides a gentle, silvery background against which to place blue, pink, yellow or mauve flowers. Used in small town gardens, it provides a lightener for dark corners or a division between

Pittosporum tobira

groups or colors, blending as it does with all spectrums. Originating in the Mediterranean and Portugal, it has always been a favorite for topiary work; it can be turned into a standard to make an elegant accent on a terrace. Against a wall or trellis, it can be trimmed to form a pillar or allowed to spread outward. It is excellent when positioned near glass doors where it frames a view without darkening the room inside.
Size H and S: to 10 ft. **Aspect** Flourishes in all aspects. **Planting partners** *Artemisia* 'Powis Castle,' *Salvia farinacea* 'Victoria,' *Clematis* 'Maidwell Hall'; summer bedding plants such as *Pelargonium*, *Impatiens*, *Petunia*.

Privet see *Ligustrum*

Star magnolia see *Magnolia stellata*

Climbers

Climbers provide a vital dimension to the container garden, giving the importance and impact only height can create. They afford shelter and privacy and a chance to grow yet more plants in a limited space.

Clematis armandii

While most clematis appear lukewarm about contained life, this vigorous evergreen species is an exception. It likes the mild walls provided by city gardens and clambers and spreads successfully from large containers and even smallish raised beds. It has large, dark green leaves and bears swathes of scented, saucer-shaped flowers in early spring; 'Snow Drift' has pure white flowers, larger than the species, while 'Apple Blossom' has pink and white flowers and is less rampant. Prune if necessary by removing the entire shoot when flowering is over, and tie in new growth lightly; remove any dead leaves throughout the year. If you are forced to be ruthless and chop it right back, it will refurbish itself. Propagate by stem cuttings in summer; plant in rich compost and mulch well in spring.
Size H and S: to over 30 ft. **Aspect** Needs a sheltered, south- or west-facing position. **Planting partners** Late-flowering *Camellia*, *Daphne*, *Euphorbia*, *Magnolia stellata*, *Iberis sempervirens*, *Choisya ternata* and early spring bulbs.

Humulus lupulus 'Aureus'

Golden climbing hop see *Humulus lupulus*

Hedera
(Ivy)

Without ivies, with their versatility, ease of growing and attractive coloring and leaf shape, pot gardening would barely survive. These evergreen climbers produce two forms of growth: juvenile, which clings, and adult, which bears flowers and fruit and waves above the juvenile. Cuttings taken from the adult growth will produce rounded, bushy shrubs known as "tree ivies"; rooted pieces or cuttings from young plants are one of the easiest ways to fill containers or raised beds. However, ivies do require watching in small spaces, controlling when growing up walls and houses, and severe thinning when in pots, planters and window boxes.

Specialist catalogs reveal hundreds of ivy species and cultivars to suit every aspect and taste. *H. helix*, native to Europe, is the hardiest ivy, with glossy, dark green leaves, sometimes with silver marking along veins; it is good for ground cover or walls. The smaller-leaved cultivars of this species are considered tender but appear hardy in sheltered or mild areas. 'Buttercup' is a useful golden form; 'Glacier' has silver-gray leaves, edged with white; 'Goldheart,' whose dark green, pointed leaves retain their cheerful gold centers even in shade, forms an excellent background to lighter greens and yellow, blue or white flowers. 'Sagittifolia' has five-lobed, arrow-shaped leaves; 'Silver Queen' presents grayish leaves with blue-green centers, widely edged with cream, and turning attractively pink-tinged in winter. 'Green Ripple' has small, jagged-lobed leaves and 'Manda's Crested' curly green leaves that color in a random manner, giving a lively and interesting effect.

Large cultivars, such as *H. canariensis variegata* 'Gloire de Marengo,' provide excellent trellis covering for roofs and balconies or for a trellis-covered trash-can screen for city front gardens; planted in a raised bed with a wall to itself, it will cover it totally and impenetrably, its lower stems becoming as thick as trees. *H. colchica dentata* is dark green, large-leaved and a good wall coverer; 'Variegata' has creamy yellow and pale green added to the leaves.

All ivies need regular feeding from spring to early autumn; those grown on walls or fences should be cut back in spring, with too-long growths shortened in summer. When used round the edges of tubs or urns, aim for long, dangling growth with as little supporting root as possible, otherwise you have massive rootballs filling every available cranny.
Size to 33 ft. **Aspect** Green-leaved ivies are shade-tolerant and do well against a north-facing wall; those with variegated or golden leaves prefer more light. **Planting partners** Variegated ivies contrast well with dark evergreen plantings; plain forms are good with variegated or light green plants, such as a variegated *Rhamnus*.

Humulus lupulus
'Aureus'
(Golden climbing hop)

This hardy, fast-growing, deciduous climber has hairy stems and yellowish, lobed leaves. It looks pretty placed beside an arch or ornamental gazebo and will twine attractively round it, covering it by mid-summer, and dying down in the autumn. It looks good set behind an evergreen hedge against a wall, balanced with *Lysimachia nummularia* 'Aurea' (creeping Jenny) in front. Its dangling hops, produced in summer, hang below the bright gold leaves; the hops can be dried for winter decoration. It is easily propagated by root cuttings or seeds.
Size H: 10–20 ft. **Aspect** Grow in sun or semi-shade. **Planting partners** *Alchemilla mollis*; grow over an arch with *Cobaea scandens* on the other side.

Ivy see *Hedera*

Potato vine see *Solanum jasminoides*

Solanum jasminoides
'Album'
(Potato vine)

This superb evergreen climber has a manageable size and spread and is indispensable for a sheltered, sunny contained garden. Its glossy, pale green leaves look good all year round and the delicate white flowers are produced abundantly from early sum-

mer till early winter. It is a good plant to site where you can look down upon it, when the charming white stars pour through an evergreen background. It can be grown through another shrub, such as a *Pittosporum*, *Rhamnus* or *Myrtus* (myrtle), or alone against a sunny wall. Gardeners with exposed terraces could grow it in an ornamental pot for over-wintering indoors. Cut back any shoots damaged by frost in spring, and remove any weak, unwanted growth. Propagate from cuttings taken in summer, in case of disaster; over-winter them under glass and place outside the following spring; young plants take a couple of years to grow but produce flowers even when young.
Size H and S: 10–15 ft. **Aspect** Needs a sheltered, sunny position, ideally a southwest-facing wall. **Planting partners** *Trachelospermum jasminoides*, *Pittosporum tobira*, *Cistus*, *Zinnia* 'Envy,' *Felicia*, *Convolvulus cneorum*, *Salvia horminum*, *Argyranthemum*, *Lavandula*, *Myrtus*, *Rhamnus*.

Clematis armandii 'Snow Drift'

Perennials

Agapanthus Headbourne Hybrid

Perennials are a challenging group to fit into the container world but their versatility ensures them a place. You have to be ruthless in their selection, aiming for good staying power, with foliage and flower interest, good shape or architectural line.

African lily see *Agapanthus*

Agapanthus
(African lily)

These decorative, clump-forming perennials have strappy leaves and tall, erect stems carrying large trumpet-shaped flowers in summer. Headbourne Hybrids are hardier than the species and the flowers are in shades of pale to deep blue, and white. These plants are excellent for decorative use, especially in large pots around a pool or near water; a group of mixed colors on a large, sunny terrace would be magical. Feed and water well during the growing season; cut spent flowers to the ground, removing all yellow leaves. Grow from seed sown in spring, flowering in two to three years; easily divided in late spring.

Size H: 2–2½ ft.; S: 20 in. **Aspect** Requires a sunny, sheltered position. **Planting partners** Best alone, rather than in a mixed planting.

Campanula poscharskyana

Since there are many campanulas, all of which make delightful container plants, it might seem perverse to choose one species described as "rampant, extremely invasive and spreading." But because a container garden is so easily controlled, and these plants are easy to pull up, their sprawling and promiscuous habits become positively engaging, not threatening. The pretty, rounded, sharp-toothed leaves and long sprays of lavender-blue star-

shaped flowers of this perennial plant carry on from early summer to late winter, and it pops up absolutely anywhere. Any pot, occupied or not, is likely to have some endearing little seedlings clustering in corners and walls, paving and gravel all become host to colonies—and a soft mass of lavender blue is infinitely preferable to bare paving in my view. They flourish in shade and need no more than a drink, so can be allowed to colonize awkward bits at the side of a town house, for example. Where they interfere with your long-term plans they can simply be pulled out.

Size H: to 12 in.; S: 2–3 ft. **Aspect** Sun or shade. **Planting partners** *Camellia*, *Erigeron mucronatus*.

Common flax see *Linum perenne* and *Linum narbonense*

Heuchera sanguinea
'Snow Storm'

A useful, good-tempered plant that is both cheerful and long-flowering. It makes a perfect edging for raised beds. The clear, cerise-pink flowers 1 ft. high are held above prettily crinkled, rounded, pale green leaves that are mottled all over as though covered in snow. In city gardens especially, the variations of green found in variegated foliage play such a vital part that the flowers are almost secondary. This plant is easy to divide and replant.

Size H and S: 10–14 in. **Aspect** Prefers full sun. **Planting partners** *Daphne odora* 'Aureomarginata'; *Choisya ternata*; spring bulbs such as *Mus-*

cari (grape hyacinth), and *Chionodoxa*, *Tulipa*, *Petunia*.

Horned violet see *Viola cornuta*

Hosta
(Plantain lily)

The many hostas all provide excellent decorative foliage and no proper container garden with shade should be without one. Their large oval or heart-shaped leaves are ribbed and come in many shades of green as well as gray-ish-blue, and there are several cultivars with white or yellow margins; *H. fortunei* 'Albopicta' has pale green leaves with creamy yellow centers. Their flowers, although secondary, are often pretty and some are scented. They are best alone, or with two cultivars in a good-sized pot allowed to arch gracefully all around; they are excellent beside water gardens. Hostas require rich compost, being happiest in almost neat manure, and with plenty of water at all times. Their tendency to attract devouring snails is less of a problem in containers. Plant from fall to spring; divide and replant in spring. *H. ventricosa* 'Aureo-macu-lata' provides wonderful spring cheer; *H.* 'Gold standard' is a good yellow with green margins; *H. undulata* var. *univittata* produces strangely twisted leaves with white centers. Miniatures and low-growing varieties such as *H.* 'Blue Moon' and *H.* 'Ground Master' enable small-space owners to enjoy these elegant and very striking beauties.

Size H and S: from 5 in. to 5 ft. **Aspect** Needs shade. **Planting partners** Best in a pot alone but excellent beside *Acer japonica*, *Rhododendron* (azalea), *Astilbe*, or ferns.

Linum perenne and Linum narbonense
(Common flax)

These charming, sun-loving perennial plants generally die off after flowering but seed themselves profusely in open ground and can easily be raised from seed for pots. They have narrow, gray-green leaves and rich blue, saucer-shaped flowers borne from early summer till early fall. The delicacy of these plants is enhanced by the flowers' tendency to "dance," or to wave and tremble in a breeze. If you go on vacation in mid-summer, cut the stems back to half, and more flowers will greet you on your return.

Size H: 12–18 in.; S: 12–24 in. **Aspect** Prefers sun. **Planting partners** Any plant that enjoys sun.

Plantain lily see *Hosta*

Viola cornuta
'Belmont Blue'
(Horned violet)

Clumps of violas, the true perennial relative of pansies, can be tucked in the front of any mixed planting, provided they have a reasonable depth

of compost (4–6 in.) and are kept well watered to counteract the drying effect of roots all round. The flowers of this cultivar are a marvelously clear sky-blue, and they are borne freely throughout spring and early summer, requiring daily dead-heading. Cut right back to the ground in mid-summer, top-dress with good compost, and the plant will refurnish itself and flower again profusely. Spray monthly with Benlate® according to the manufacturer's instructions, to prevent pansy sickness, which causes leaves to wilt and turn yellow and the plant eventually to rot. Easily grown from cuttings taken in summer, grown on and planted in position in spring.

Size H: 4–8 in.; S: 12–16 in. **Aspect** Sun or shade. **Planting partners** Standard *Fuchsia*, *Argyranthemum frutescens*, *Viburnum tinus* 'Variegatum,' *Hebe × andersonii* 'Variegata,' *Pelargonium* 'Highfield's Pearl.'

Heuchera sanguinea 'Snow Storm'

Bedding plants

Bedding plants provide the highlights in a container garden. Their short lifespan, compared with trees or shrubs, allows for dramatic color choices, spectacular mixtures and wonderful scented corners. Because the range is so wide, you can experiment with new plants and different combinations, enlarging your horizons and improving your selection each year.

Impatiens Novette Series

Argyranthemum

(Marguerite or Daisy bush)
These tender, evergreen shrubs are often grown as summer bedding. Their white, daisy flowers with yellow centers are produced from very early summer until the first cold spell. 'Mary Wootton' has pale pink, double flowers; 'Jamaica Primrose' flowers are a soft yellow; 'Powder Puff' is double, very pale pink and small; 'Vancouver' is a deeper pink. The delicate, fern-like leaves are either bright green or silver, the silver-leaved cultivar being the finer. They can be trained into standards, when they become a spectacular addition to any sunny courtyard or balcony, and are excellent in sunny window boxes, amongst pelargoniums, petunias and lobelias. The secret of continuous flowering is to check the plants constantly, never letting them dry out and removing any flowers with the slightest hint of fading, right back to the growing point, where new emergent buds can just be seen. Given winter protection, they will continue to flower endlessly, requiring gradual drying-off to enforce rest, before the renewed activity in spring. Should the plants dry out, you should cut back to the main stem and feed well; this should cause new growth to appear.
Size H: to 3 ft.; S: to 2½ ft. **Aspect** Prefers a sunny position. **Planting partners** Yellow with *Hebe* 'Bowles' Variety,' *Phormium tenax* 'Cream Delight,' *Salvia farinacea* 'Victoria'; white with *Felicia*, *Heliotropum*, trailing *Verbena*, pots of *Linum perenne*, a mass of *Osteospermum ecklonis*.

Begonia

These cheerful and widely grown bedding plants have a lush opulence. They are invaluable for hanging baskets in some shade, with colors ranging from white to red and all hues of pink and orange in between, and leaves that vary from fresh, bright green to bronze. They are tuberous in *Begonia pendula* Non-Stop F_1 Hybrids and fibrous-rooted in *Begonia semperflorens*. The tubers can be started into growth in warmth, and stored over winter in frost-free conditions. Seeds for both types can be sown under glass.
Size H: 10–12 in.; S: 12 in. **Aspect** Prefers some shade. **Planting partners** *Fuchsia*, *Petunia*, *Lobelia*, *Pelargonium*.

Daisy bush see *Argyranthemum*

Felicia amelloides

These evergreen sub-shrubs carry marvelously bright blue daisy flowers well above the foliage all summer and into winter, in good weather. The great charm of this plant is its fresh and sparkling character, and its habit of tumbling down, then turning up. It looks its best in a raised urn or pot on a pedestal, over which it can spread and tumble. It never becomes blowsy as summer progresses, as some of our bedding plants do; given regular deadheading, it will brighten a sunny terrace until severe frost. Felicias can be grown from seed or by cuttings in summer. If winter shelter can be provided, they will flower and spread more vigorously the following year. **Size** H: 18 in.; S: 12–18 in. **Aspect** Sunny. **Planting partners** *Cordyline australis*, variegated *Buxus*, *Hebe*, *Origanum aureum*, *Lysimachia nummularia* 'Aurea,' *Viola*, *Phygelius aequalis* 'Yellow Trumpet.'

Flowering tobacco plant see
Nicotiana

Fuchsia

The members of this family of deciduous or evergreen shrubs form graceful shapes; they enjoy life in hanging baskets and are easily trained into standards. Their bell-shaped, tubular flowers are often bicolored, in a range of color combinations from white to violet, pink of all shades, reds from crimson through to orange. Their showy flowers, coupled with their rather artificial, stagy appearance, make them prime candidates for containers.

The plants have been widely hybridized since their first introduction, producing hundreds of different cultivars. A few are hardy but the majority are tender and are best treated as summer bedding plants, given protection in winter and raised from cuttings. These take with ridiculous ease, stuck in a jar of water, or twiggy prunings put directly in a pot. Most cultivars flower for four or five months, from summer until winter. They require good compost, plenty of humus,

some bonemeal, and regular feeding and watering all summer long.

The most decorative for permanent planting is *F. magellanica gracilis* 'Versicolor' (H: up to 10 ft.; S: up to 6½ ft.), with lovely grayish-green leaves, tinged with pink, arching out in a constant waterfall, and small, delicate red and purple flowers lasting all summer. Other good cultivars include: 'Graf Witte,' a graceful spreader with yellow-green leaves and pink and purple flowers; 'Brilliant,' bushy and vigorous with large, single, cerise and purple flowers over a long season; 'Lena,' reliable and compact, with semi-double, pale pink and purple flowers; 'Mrs Popple,' somewhat dumpy but always excellent in hanging baskets, with its bright scarlet and purple flowers.
Size H and S: from 16 in.–10 ft. **Aspect** Prefers a sheltered, slightly shaded position. **Planting partners** *Lilium*, *Hedera*, *Petunia*.

Geranium see *Pelargonium*

Impatiens

This group of tender perennial plants is grown as summer bedding chiefly for its dazzling range of flower colors—white, pink, scarlet, crimson, orange or maroon—single, double, striped or bicolored. They are invaluable for placing in shade and, provided they are never allowed to dry out, will carry on flowering all summer without a pause. Deservedly

Felicia amelloides

popular, these reliable, unfussy, long-lasting little plants provide a trouble-free answer to owners of a dark, sunless courtyard.

Many selections have been raised, including Imp (9 in. high), in single colors in white, rose, carmine, orange, scarlet and violet, and *I. petersiana* (to 3 ft.) with bronze-red, pointed leaves and large carmine flowers. I prefer either an all-white scheme, or totally mixed, with every shade jammed in together in a wild riot of color, but they can be blended with most color schemes in any position that remains moist and are splendid for hanging baskets. Grow them in good compost and feed well. Propagate from cuttings taken from spring through to early autumn; they can also be rooted in water, and grown from seed.
Size H and S: see above. **Aspect** Tolerates even deep shade. **Planting partners** *Camellia*, *Pieris*, *Acer palmatum* cultivars, ferns.

Lobelia erinus

In its trailing or upright form, with small flowers in shades of blue, pink, purple and white, this must be one of the most frequently planted of all summer container plants. The compact form is good for raised beds but its trailing cultivar adds enormously to container life, whether pouring from hanging baskets, mixed with petunias and helichrysum, edging raised beds, or making a rounded waterfall out of a window box. I find the pale blue form most decorative, but the cultivar 'Crystal Palace,' with dark blue flowers and bronze foliage, is also attractive. Should neglect cause it to dry out, cut it back, feed it and wait a few weeks —it will refurbish itself readily and your blue cloud will carry on all summer. Lobelia can be raised from seed planted under glass in early spring, but in cities it is usually bought as seedlings.

Size H: 8 in.; S: 4–6 in. **Aspect** Prefers sun. **Planting partners** *Osteospermum, Senecio maritima, Zinnia,* white *Petunia* or *Pelargonium, Linaria, Salvia farinacea* 'Victoria.'

Marguerite see *Argyranthemum*

Nicotiana
(Flowering tobacco plant)

These perennials are normally grown as showy annuals for pot work, since they flower all summer in shades of soft pink, cream, lime green, red and purple, and smell delicious, particularly when they open in the evenings. They are a useful plant to combat too many "daisy" flowers, their pointed, tubular flower shapes making a good contrast, and their slim height is valuable among dumpy "billowers" such as petunias or pelargoniums. The dwarf cultivars and hybrids are better for window boxes and small containers, although scentless. *N. langsdorfii* (H: 3–5 ft.; S: 12 in.) has spectacular yellowy green tubular flowers that are both architectural and decorative. It looks good in a prominent position, with a frill of *Senecio maritima* 'Silver Dust' around its base. *N. sylvestris* produces fragrant white tubes in late summer, making a great impact; it is as tall as *N. langsdorfii* but thicker in growth.

Size H. and S: see above. **Aspect** Prefers sun but tolerates some shade. **Planting partners** *Hebe, Viola, Verbena, Bellis perennis.*

Pelargonium
(Geranium)

No container gardener can ignore pelargoniums. A glance in any specialist catalog will show speckled, finger-flowered, double and semi-double, cactus-flowered, stellar, tulip-flowered, scented-leaved, ornamental foliage, dwarf, miniature, trailing, regal—and many other cultivars. Their range of shades and styles is infinitely wider than the ubiquitous bright red seen blazing fiercely down from municipal plantings everywhere: they repay study and an adventurous approach. The trailing, ivy-leaved pelargoniums make good hanging basket and window box dwellers; and the regals can be trained into standards, given winter protection. These tender sub-shrubs are known as tender evergreen greenhouse plants in temperate climates and treated as summer bedding by those without glass. They are easily rooted from cuttings taken in summer, or from over-wintered plants in early spring; grow from seed under glass in very early spring. Despite being sun-lovers, they will survive and flower quite well in less perfect positions, even enduring drought. They prefer a compost that is not too rich but benefit from summer feeding.

Size H and S: to 2 ft. **Aspect** Prefers sun. **Planting partners** *Lobelia erinus, Hedera, Helichrysum petiolare.*

Salvia farinacea
'Victoria'

This semi-hardy perennial, generally grown as a half-hardy annual, is a treasure. Its long, violet-blue flower spikes are borne well above the soft-green, pointed leaves; its violet-blue stems make a group both striking and versatile. It can be raised from seed, requiring a start under glass if it is to flower the same year, or propagated from cuttings that need to be over-wintered under glass. It requires good compost to flourish.

Size H: 18 in.; S: 12 in. **Aspect** Sunny position. **Planting partners** *Phormium tenax* 'Yellow Wave,' *Nigella damascena* 'Persian Jewels,' *Molucella laevis, Dimorphotheca,* white *Petunia,* all silver foliage plants.

Bulbs

Daffodil see *Narcissus*

Lilium regale

No container garden should be without at least one pot of these marvelous elegant plants. This stem-rooting lily is easy to grow, producing its superb trumpet-shaped, scented flowers in mid-summer, which are white, with sulphur-yellow centers, shaded deep rose outside. *L.r.* 'Album' is pure white. Their magical perfume wafts through a window the moment a bud opens and continues until the last petal drops. They require plenty of water during their growth cycle, never being allowed to dry out, but behave with great docility and dependability. In pots the bulbs eventually dwindle and after five or six years produce only single blooms, against their initial 15–20. They are easily grown from seed, flowering within two or three years, or can be increased by growing on the bulbils formed around the parent; these can be set in seed trays and potted up when large enough. If ordering from a grower, inspect the bulbs carefully before planting to see that they are plump and not dried out. If choosing from a nursery, the best time is autumn, planting them without delay and covering the pots with chopped bracken fern if frost threatens. Three bulbs per pot is the recommended ratio but I prefer to use much larger containers, such as an old copper or ornamental stone or terra-cotta, and to mix them with compatible foliage. Plant in a rich compost, incorporating peat-type improver and leaf mold.

Watch for early growth, and spray with soapy water against aphids, a constant predator during their entire life cycle. In a single pot, replace the compost annually, in autumn.
Size H: 3–5 ft. **Planting depth** 6–9 in., and 4–6 in. apart. **Aspect** Needs sun. **Planting partners** *Artemisia*, *Linum perenne*, *L. narbonense*, *Fuchsia magellanica gracilis*, *Helichrysum petiolare*, white *Petunia*.

Narcissus
(Daffodil)

Botanically, there are many divisions and sub-divisions governing these invaluable bulbs, but the names of the cultivars that have proved reliable for long-term pot work are all that matter for our purposes. 'February Gold' and 'February Silver' are the most trustworthy pair, appearing year after year in window boxes, albeit somewhat diminished. Their bulbs are large, considering their small height, but the clear yellow petals and slightly darker cup of 'February Gold' are superb, as is the pure white of 'February Silver.' Others in this dwarf group include 'Jack Snipe,' creamy white with a yellow trumpet, and 'Tête-à-Tête,' multi-flowered and butter-yellow. Another group with swept-back petals contains the tall, white-flowered 'Thalia,' the lemon-yellow 'Hawera,' which is small and looks good with grape hyacinths, and 'April Tears,' a deeper yellow. 'Cheerfulness' comes in both white and yellow forms and will grow with little or no sun, flowering later with button flowers, 12 in. high.

Lilium regale

Many bulbs have a particular affinity with pots and have been grown in this way since their discovery. The scope of bulbs is vast and one of the marvelous aspects is their reliability, at least for the first year—the challenge coming in the following years.

Another taller one, 'Winston Churchill,' 15 in. high, is scented and sturdy. *Narcissus triandrus triandrus* (Angel Tears) is a tiny, pale, droopy-flowered candidate for an alpine trough or miniature garden; 'Binkie,' lemon yellow, produces many flowers per bulb.
Size H: 6–15 in. **Aspect** Sun or light shade. **Planting partners** Most spring flowers.

Index

Plant hardiness zones

This hardiness map will help you to establish which plants are most suitable for your garden. The zones 2–11 are based on the average annual minimum temperature for each zone and appear after the plant entry in the index. The lower number indicates the northernmost zone in which the plant can survive the winter, and the higher number, the most southerly area in which it will perform consistently. Plant zones 2–3 are suitable for central Canada and zones 4–6 for coastal and southern Canada.

ZONE 2	−50° TO −40° F
ZONE 3	−40° TO −30°
ZONE 4	−30° TO −20°
ZONE 5	−20° TO −10°
ZONE 6	−10° to 0°
ZONE 7	0° TO 10°
ZONE 8	10° TO 20°
ZONE 9	20° TO 30°
ZONE 10	30° TO 40°
ZONE 11	ABOVE 40°

Acknowledgments

The publisher thanks the following photographers and organizations for their kind permission to reproduce the photographs in this book:

1 Marijke Heuff (Sijtje Sturman); 2–3 Philippe Perdereau; 4–5 Jerry Harpur; 6–7 Jerry Harpur (Thomasina Tarling); 8 Gary Rogers; 9 Clive Nichols; 10 above Jerry Harpur (Meadowbrook Farm, Philadelphia); 10 below Philippe Perdereau; 11 Jacqui Hurst/Boys Syndication; 12 left Jacqui Hurst/Boys Syndication; 12 right Andrew Lawson; 13 Robert César/Agence Top; 14–16 Marianne Majerus; 17 left Marijke Heuff (Nursery Overhagen, Holland); 17 right Jerry Harpur/Elizabeth Whiting and Associates; 18 above left Marijke Heuff (Nursery de Rhulenhof, Holland); 18 below left Guy Bouchet/Garden Picture Library; 18 right Michèle Lamontagne; 19 above Annette Schreiner; 19 below S & O Mathews; 20 Jerry Harpur/Elizabeth Whiting and Associates; 21 Marijke Heuff (Priona Gardens, Holland); 22 above Gary Rogers; 22 below Heather Angel/Biofotos; 23 above Jerry Harpur; 23 below Christine Ternynck; 25 Juliette Wade; 26 Michael Boys/Boys Syndication; 28 Photos Horticultural; 31 Photos Horticultural; 33 Gary Rogers; 35 Philippe Perdereau; 36 Clive Nichols; 40–1 Philippe Perdereau; 42 Michael Boys/Boys Syndication; 43 above S & O Mathews; 43 below Philippe Perdereau; 44 Philippe Perdereau; 45 left Andrew Lawson; 45 above right John Miller; 45 below right Marianne Majerus; 46 Brian Carter/Garden Picture Library; 47 Michèle Lamontagne; 48 Andrew Lawson; 49 Christine Ternynck; 51 Michael Boys/Boys Syndication; 54 Jerry Harpur (designer: Maggie Geiger); 55 Clive Frost/Vogue Living; 56 left Annette Schreiner; 56 right Jerry Harpur (Thomasina Tarling); 57 Marijke Heuff (Mr. O. Hoek, Holland); 58–9 Gary Rogers; 62 left Ron Sutherland/Garden Picture Library; 62 right Jerry Harpur (designer: Simon Fraser); 63 Philippe Perdereau; 64 left John Glover/Garden Picture Library; 64 right Davis Russell/Garden Picture Library; 65 Philippe Perdereau; 66 Photos Horticultural; 67 Marianne Majerus; 70 S & O Mathews; 71 Andrew Lawson; 72–3 Jerry Harpur (designer: Beth Chatto); 74 Gary Rogers; 75 above Philippe Perdereau; 75 below Andrew Lawson; 76 left Tania Midgley; 76 above right Tim Sandall; 76 below right Photos Horticultural; 77 left Clive Nichols; 77 right Eric Crichton; 80 Jerry Harpur (Thomasina Tarling); 81 Christine Ternynck; 82 Annette Schreiner; 83 Vaughan Fleming/Garden Picture Library; 86 above Brigitte Thomas/Garden Picture Library; 86 below Andrew Lawson; 87 Andrew Lawson; 90 Annette Schreiner; 91 left Gary Rogers; 91 right Guy Bouchet; 92 Gary Rogers; 93 Michèle Lamontagne; 94 Clive Nichols; 95 Gary Rogers; 96 above Andrew Lawson; 96 below Jerry Harpur (Chelsea 1991 Royal Borough of Kensington & Chelsea Gardens); 97 John Miller; 98 Morley Read/Garden Picture Library; 99 Michael Boys/Boys Syndication; 100 Annette Schreiner; 101 Jerry Harpur (Malcolm Hillier); 102–3 Heather Angel/Biofotos; 104–6 Andrew Lawson; 107 Juliette Wade; 108–9 Clive Nichols; 110 Tania Midgley; 112 Garden Picture Library; 113–5 Photos Horticultural; 116 Heather Angel/Biofotos; 118 Marijke Heuff (Garden Mien Ruys); 120 Michael Boys/Boys Syndication.

The publisher also thanks: Vanessa Courtier and Helen Ridge.